You Are
Beloved

BOBBY SCHULLER

You Are
Beloved

LIVING IN THE FREEDOM
OF GOD'S GRACE, MERCY, AND LOVE

NELSON
BOOKS

An Imprint of Thomas Nelson

Published in Nashville, Tennessee, by Nelson Books, an imprint of Thomas Nelson. Nelson Books and Thomas Nelson are registered trademarks of HarperCollins Christian Publishing, Inc.

Published in association with Yates & Yates, www.yates2.com.

Thomas Nelson titles may be purchased in bulk for educational, business, fund-raising, or sales promotional use. For information, please e-mail SpecialMarkets@ThomasNelson.com.

Unless otherwise noted, Scripture quotations are taken from the Holy Bible, New International Version®, NIV®. Copyright © 1973, 1978, 1984, 2011 by Biblica, Inc.® Used by permission of Zondervan. All rights reserved worldwide. www.Zondervan.com. The "NIV" and "New International Version" are trademarks registered in the United States Patent and Trademark Office by Biblica, Inc.®

Scripture quotations marked THE MESSAGE are from *The Message*. Copyright © by Eugene H. Peterson 1993, 1994, 1995, 1996, 2000, 2001, 2002. Used by permission of NavPress. All rights reserved. Represented by Tyndale House Publishers, Inc.

Scripture quotations marked NASB are from New American Standard Bible®. Copyright © 1960, 1962, 1963, 1968, 1971, 1972, 1973, 1975, 1977, 1995 by The Lockman Foundation. Used by permission. (www.Lockman.org)

Scripture quotations marked BSB are taken from the Holy Bible, Berean Study Bible (BSB). Copyright © 2016 by Bible Hub. Used by permission. All rights reserved worldwide.

Scripture quotations marked KJV are taken from the King James Version of the Bible.

Any Internet addresses, phone numbers, or company or product information printed in this book are offered as a resource and are not intended in any way to be or to imply an endorsement by Thomas Nelson, nor does Thomas Nelson vouch for the existence, content, or services of these sites, phone numbers, companies, or products beyond the life of this book.

ISBN 978-1-4002-0168-6 (HC)
ISBN 978-1-4002-0169-3 (eBook)
ISBN 978-1-4002-0791-6 (IE)

Library of Congress Cataloging-in-Publication Data

Names: Schuller, Bobby, 1981- author.
Title: You are beloved : living in the freedom of God's grace, mercy, and love / Bobby Schuller.
Description: Nashville : Thomas Nelson, 2018. | Includes bibliographical references.
Identifiers: LCCN 2017053064 | ISBN 9781400201686
Subjects: LCSH: God (Christianity)--Love.
Classification: LCC BT140 .S379 2018 | DDC 248.4--dc23 LC record available at https://lccn.loc.gov/2017053064

Printed in the United States of America

18 19 20 21 22 LSC 10 9 8 7 6 5 4 3 2 1

To my two beloved children, Haven and Cohen,
who taught me the depth of the Father's love.

CONTENTS

INTRODUCTION

On Forming the Creed of the Beloved

Henri Nouwen

Early in my seminary education I had a brief love affair with the discipline of philosophy—in particular with the nineteenth-century Danish philosopher Søren Kierkegaard. He was far ahead of his time and was called "post-Freudian" by intellectual giants such as Ernest Becker, even though Kierkegaard died the year before Freud was born. Kierkegaard, who was a devout Christian, wrote directly to the individual and her heart. The first time I read *Fear and Trembling* I struggled not to weep.

It was not long after that I read a book incidentally dedicated to "Henri Nouwen: Our Generation's Kierkegaard." I thought to myself, *Who is this Nouwen guy?*

As it turned out, Henri Nouwen was a Catholic priest and a bestselling author. He is one of the few Christian authors who, like Billy Graham, was loved by both the most liberal and most conservative of Christians. He could give the same message to the two Christian groups who hated each other, and both would receive his words with joy. Though he had an amazing following and was a professor at both Harvard and Yale, Nouwen spent the last years of his life caring for the intellectually disabled people of the L'Arche community in Toronto. He was a living saint.

Of course I didn't know this when I saw his name in that book. I just thought, *I wonder what it would be like to read a book by our generation's Kierkegaard?*

I went down to Barnes & Noble, grabbed Nouwen's work *Journey of the Prodigal Son*, and sat for what I imagined would be a short time in the café. Several hours later I had nearly finished the book and was deeply touched by the rawness of how Nouwen connected my heart with that of Jesus. I began reading all of his works. They all had something in common. They were very simple—anyone could read them and enjoy them—yet they had incredible depth, emotion, and spiritual power in their simplicity.

As I became a bigger fan of Nouwen, I grew sad that I was never able to meet him before he died. In fact, I wasn't quite sure what he looked like or even sounded like. That is until, by chance, while visiting the office of another pastor at the Crystal Cathedral, I saw on his bookshelf three VHS tapes labeled *Henri Nouwen*, *Being the Beloved*, and *Hour of Power*.

"What are these?" I asked my colleague, pointing to the tapes.

"Oh, those? That's that Catholic priest who came and preached at the cathedral."

"Henri Nouwen?" I exclaimed. "He preached here?"

"Oh, yeah. He and your grandpa were dear friends. You can have those if you want them. They're pretty good."

That night I heard perhaps the most important sermon of my life. In it Nouwen gave the clearest picture of grace I've ever heard:

> *You're not what you do.*
> *You're not what you have.*
> *You're not what people say about you.*
> *You are the beloved of God.*

He said this over and over, showing how building your life on what you do, what you have, or what others say about you will lead you to ruin, but building your life and character on the love of God in Christ Jesus will lead to serenity and salvation. (Incidentally this was one of only a few taped sermons Nouwen ever gave, and he died of a heart attack the following year. I've posted the sermon on YouTube.)

This is how the Creed of the Beloved began. As a spiritual discipline, for several months I would say these words before times of prayer and reflection:

> I'm not what I do. (*breathe*)
> I'm not what I have. (*breathe*)
> I'm not what people say about me. (*breathe*)
> I am the beloved of God.

Saying these words to myself as a daily practice pulled me out of the stressed-out patterns of this world, of trying to prove myself, of feeling rejected and not enough, and brought me into the easy rhythms of grace. I was training my will and character around the love of God in Christ Jesus and not around the fickle opinions of others. It was during this time I experienced one of the greatest breakthroughs in my relationship with God.

Dallas Willard

My love for Nouwen was ultimately my doorway into the world of Christian spiritual formation, inevitably leading me to the godfather of that tribe: Dallas Willard. I remember seeing people in seminary carrying around this thick book with two pencil-sketched pears on the cover called *The Divine Conspiracy*. Eventually I got a copy of my own, got about twelve pages in, and flung it across my room.

"Boring," I said aloud, annoyed.

Unlike Henri Nouwen, Dallas Willard was not simple in his approach. A professor of philosophy at the University of Southern California, Dallas spent hours making sure every word he wrote was perfect for communicating his ideas. He regularly asked people who enjoyed his works to not cite him when they quoted him. I originally interpreted this as his generosity and desire to be humble, but as I got to know him better, I wondered if this was more that he didn't want people to use his work to make a bigger point he wouldn't agree with. He was a semantic perfectionist.

The problem with *Divine Conspiracy* was not that it was boring, but rather that Dallas was using terms I was not familiar with—ideas like "the kingdom of God." It was after reading some of his essays and hearing him lecture on occasion that I finally returned to *Divine Conspiracy*. This time, being more familiar with his terminology, I blazed through it. Though I adore Henri Nouwen's work, Willard's *Divine Conspiracy* is the one book (second only to the Bible) that has had the greatest impact on my life and ministry. It is not boring at all, just difficult.

Dallas believed that many pastors and Christians today have drifted from the mandate of Jesus to become his apprentices and enter his world, the kingdom of God. Dallas believed that faith was a practice, not just an intellectual belief. He taught that to be an apprentice of Jesus was not about trying harder to follow the rules, but rather about engaging in spiritual disciplines such as fasting, silence and solitude, or memorizing and meditating on the Psalms in order to train the individual will (the heart) in the direction of God's will. Only then would we walk in the easy yoke of Jesus, yielding spiritual results.

He spent a lot of time talking about the nervousness of our culture, always encouraging Christians to stop hurrying and stop worrying so much, to live every day with the serenity of the kingdom of the heavens at the forefront of our minds.

Through my friends Michael Bischof and Bill Gaultiere, I was able to meet Dallas and develop a friendship with him. He agreed to mentor me, and for about a year I visited him in his office at USC. Those visits were some of the greatest memories of my ministry—like sitting with Jesus. My brief mentoring was cut short when Dallas contracted cancer and died shortly after.

He was always so kind, never nervous or in a hurry, and always willing to listen. I remember one Sunday morning when we were interviewing him in my little church, Tree of Life. A sign in the back of the hall fell over onto our hardwood dance floor. It made a shocking popping sound, like a balloon or a gun going off. Watching the video later, I saw that everyone, including the three pastors on stage, jumped or even stood. Dallas didn't even move. He was always calm. He was forever saying things such as, "Hurry is the great enemy of the spiritual life in our day," and "You can't have compassion for your near-dweller and be in a hurry."

It was because of Dallas's teachings that I rolled into my personal creed:

> You don't have to worry. (*breathe*)
> You don't have to hurry. (*breathe*)
> You can trust your friend Jesus and share his love with the world.

Emotional Energy from Practicing the Creed

I grew up in a fishing family. Every summer we practically lived on our fishing boat, going up and down the California coast looking for a nice dinner and a little sport. Often I would drive the boat, even when I was a kid. We had this big stainless-steel steering wheel, but no one ever used it. Instead, we drove the boat with this little dial for the autopilot. That way we could allow the computer to keep us on course instead of just eyeballing it. When we'd want to change direction, we'd turn the dial just one degree. You wouldn't even feel the boat move. But over a couple of hours that one-degree change would have you miles away from where you would have been.

Practicing this creed in my life was like changing the dial on my life by one degree. At first I didn't really notice any change. But over time I saw how, by training and aligning my mind with the Word of God through praying this creed, I found a deep sense of rootedness. I was connecting deeply with others and finding the strength to be vulnerable. I was giving up my need to control and to be perceived well by everyone, and I was keeping important emotional boundaries. In short, I was becoming a healthier person.

As I will mention later in the book, the happy side effect of this rhythm was the amount of godly energy I got from this training. I didn't realize how much my worrying and hurrying, people pleasing, addiction to adrenaline, and chasing after trophies and money was robbing my life of joy and a full spiritual battery. Letting go of those things helped me use what energy I had to focus on what really gives me life.

I'm hesitant to use the term *energy* because it can come off a bit "new age with a twist of Oprah." But I can think of no other word to describe what I received from this creed. The word *energy* is found throughout the Bible, though it is usually translated as "work" or "power."

The English word *energy* actually originates in the Greek *en* ("within") and *ergon* ("work"), which form three versions of the term *energy* found in the Bible: *energéma*, *energeia*, and *energéo*. The first, *energéma*, is usually translated as the "results" of God's power for those who live by faith. Paul used it when talking about the spiritual gifts in 1 Corinthians 12:6 when he said, "There are different kinds of working [*energéma*—results, powers, workings], but in all of them and in everyone it is the same God at work."

Similarly, the second version, *energeia*, is defined by *Strong's Concordance* as "God's energy, which transitions the believer from point to point in His plan." This energy is often translated as "working." Paul pairs it with another word, *dunamis*, meaning "power," in Ephesians 3:7, talking about his conversion: "I became a servant of this gospel by the gift of God's grace given me through the working [*energeia*—working, energy] of his power [*dunamis*—power, might, strength]."

The third and final kind of use is *energéo*, the verb that means "to energize," like an electrical current energizing a wire. It's God's miraculous power. In Eugene Peterson's translation of Philippians 2:13, he conveys Paul's use of *energéo* as "That energy is *God's* energy, an energy deep within you, God himself willing and working at what will give him the most pleasure" (THE MESSAGE).

In short, God does not want us to do his work on an empty battery. Rather, he wants to energize us through connecting deeply with him and with other believers. The Creed of the Beloved is a biblical and practical way to remove many of the lies of the Enemy and help you tap into the godly energy, joy, life, and power found in the kingdom of God. Everything in this work is firmly rooted in Scripture and will get you on track to having godly power.

THE CREED OF THE BELOVED

When I discover who I am, I'll be free.
—Ralph Ellison, *Invisible Man*

You Are Seen Deeply and Loved

You belong and you are wanted, just as you are and not as you should be. There is no one like you in the whole world. You're doing better than you think. More people than you think love you. You are a treasure, and you have nothing to prove.

See, what I'm discovering is that my deepest need is to know I matter and belong. God made humans this way. But, because of our need to matter and belong, it is so easy to fall into the never-ending pursuit of approval and love through:

- what you do
- what you have
- what people say about you

Every day advertisers and others promise us that with a few tweaks we'll be more attractive and popular. Our peers imply that when we succeed in our goals and aspirations, our lives will count and be "one for the history books." Meanwhile churches and charities make us feel guilty and ask us to do more for them, for our children or spouse, and for the world. All of these things are great, yet every day they seem just a bit out of reach.

Perhaps you feel as though you are being pulled in a thousand directions. You feel like you are sacrificing everything but are completely out of energy and unhappy. You long for the times in your life when you had fewer worries, when you felt less pressure and stress, and you wonder if you'll ever get that life back. You daydream about an existence very different from the one you are currently experiencing—one that is fun, free, and energized. Maybe you wish you could be a kid again.

At the same time you feel a sense of shame because you didn't do as well as you thought you would. You could've been a better parent or grandparent. You could have achieved more in your career if you'd just tried a little harder. Plus you're getting older and are feeling less wanted. You promise yourself that tomorrow you're going to give it 110 percent but somewhere deep inside feel as if maybe you won't.

Don't beat yourself up, because the nasty little secret is everyone feels this way. From the wealthiest to the poorest, from the oldest to the youngest, we human beings constantly feel a sense of not being enough. We just masquerade it. We show our best to others while hiding the things that make us "unworthy" of respect and belonging. We publicly display to one another how terrific we are while secretly feeling like we're not enough.

As we compare our true, hidden self to others' public shiny versions of themselves, we run out of energy trying to keep up with one another. We wake up hoping to outpace our peers while regretting the wasted years we could have spent being happy. The net result is everyone is tired because they are hurrying to be loved. Little do they know, they already are.

You are loved by God. You always have been and you always will be. He was there when you were born, and he'll be there to catch your last breath. Your accomplishments don't matter to him as much as your smile. Your treasures only matter to him because they matter to you. You're his treasure. He also doesn't care about your reputation. He simply longs to be with you. He calls you *beloved*.

This was made real for me when I became a young father many years ago. I remember one early morning when the sun was still sleeping and I was trying to rock my little four-week-old peanut back to sleep. Looking at her, I thought, *I'd do anything for you.* I was exhausted from not sleeping, yet overwhelmed with joy just to be with her. She hadn't done anything for me. She merely was, and that was all I needed. She was and is a beloved treasure.

The great love I feel for my children is very little compared to the immense love God has for you. He calls you his beloved treasure. He's your loving Father. He is not angry with you. He is not holding a grudge against you. He simply longs to be with you and bless you. You are his. This is your identity. Discovering it makes all the difference.

There is nothing like living in the identity of the beloved. Being friends with God helps us live every day with full hearts. When we know we are his beloved, we have clear vision, good sleep, big dreams, and peace. Being the beloved gives us the strength to let go of our regrets, self-pity, and bitterness and helps us inherit an inner joy that never goes away.

The ultimate goal of this book is to teach you to have incredible energy by rooting your identity in nothing but the love of God.

You may not know this about yourself, but every part of you is crying out to connect with God and with others. You need to feel the deep, sustaining joy that comes from being seen deeply by the people who love you. You'll never be fulfilled by your trophies, entertainment, fashion, fun, or your dazzling reputation. You'll only connect with others when you are at peace with yourself and with God. Only then can you begin to show others who you truly are and know that you are worthy of respect and belonging.

This is your "why." It's the reason you do everything. In a way, it's everyone's deepest motivator: to get connected with others and with God.

I believe if you stick with me over the chapters in this book, your life will never be the same. You'll begin to see some of the ways your behaviors are coming from a lack of joy rooted in a sense of "not being enough." As you begin to believe you truly belong in God's world, you'll develop more energy, clarity of purpose, and vision for your life, and you'll cut out a lot of the useless stuff that chokes your soul.

I have developed a creed that has made this change possible for thousands of people around the world. A creed is like a prayer you say to yourself to realign your mind and heart with what really matters. If you're an American, you likely said the Pledge of Allegiance every morning at school. This patriotic creed is taught to children to help them remember what it means to be an American. In the same way, the Creed of the Beloved will help you train your mind and heart to know what it means to be the beloved of God. Over time the scriptural truths in this creed will give you an incredible sense of energy and power to succeed in every aspect of your life.

Discovering My Personal Why

In the eighties, my grandfather, Robert H. Schuller, was the most-watched religious television personality in the world on the program he started, *Hour of Power*. Every Sunday millions of people around the world looked forward to watching him preach a powerful word from the Crystal Cathedral about *possibility thinking*. Many in my generation are unfamiliar with Dr. Schuller, but no doubt he will be remembered as one of the greatest influencers of the Christian church in the twentieth century. If you've ever been to a church calling itself "seeker sensitive," you can thank him.

Of course, this meant very little to me as a kid. I simply saw him as my fishing buddy, my chubby grandpa who gave great hugs. This remained mostly true until I was about eighteen years old and was invited to go with him and five hundred members of his viewing audience to Israel.

Shortly after arriving in Jerusalem that first evening, I found myself wandering around the lobby of our hotel. I was looking at their displays of religious artifacts yet couldn't forget I was in an everyday Hyatt. I was feeling antsy and wanting to go see this famous city for the first time when, out of nowhere, a man with a bushy red beard and a big personality said, "Are you Robert Schuller?"

"Sort of," I replied. "But probably not the one you're looking for."

"You'll do," he quipped. "My name is Israel." And after a warm but brief conversation, we were off to his home.

He was a Jewish-Christian man who told me he'd had a profound encounter with God while serving in the Israeli army. It was this encounter that convinced him to become a Christian. He also proved to the Israeli government that he was a direct descendant of King David. This led to the government giving him special land just outside of the city that would have belonged to the family of David.

We walked to his home under the stars. In the warmth of the evening, he showed me a couple of dig sites, an ancient baptismal, and a little outdoor chapel he had made years ago. He shared stories about his country and what it was like growing up there. Then he stopped by a little outdoor table to make a phone call. After talking briefly with someone on the other line, he said, "The real reason I brought you up here was for this." He pushed toward me his tan-colored, seventies-looking phone. "For you," he said.

On the line, a woman introduced herself and told me her story. She said years ago she'd been married to an Eastern Orthodox priest. At first the marriage was sweet, but it wasn't long before he became violent and cold hearted. He beat her regularly and from his own religious perspective felt he had every right to do so. Having grown up in this tradition, she'd believed priests to be God's mediators, a reflection of God himself. As her then-husband abused her physically and verbally, she felt as though it was God himself abusing her, beating her.

One day, alone in her room, she turned on the TV and saw a kind-looking old man in a robe say, "God loves you and so do I!" She said he smiled right at her through the screen.

She began to watch my grandpa every week. His words gave her hope and encouragement that God really did love her and that God wanted the best for her. She believed for the first time that she deserved better than this—she deserved love and respect. She became convinced she could get out of this mess . . . somehow.

One day, as she was watching my grandpa's show on TV, the ministry offered a little cross with that same phrase—"God loves you and so do I"—engraved on it. This line meant so much to her that she gave a donation—her first to a ministry—to get it. But upon arriving in the mail, it was intercepted by her husband, who was so enraged he beat her bloody, and she ended up in the hospital. It was there, cross in hand, that she decided she would leave her husband and start a new life.

Over that tan-colored phone, I heard her say, "Now, years later, I've started a nonprofit that helps abused women all over the world. The man you are standing with is my new husband, and we are so happy. It's all because of your grandpa's words, 'God loves you and so do I.'" She continued, "Those words gave me the strength to become the woman I was called to be."

She had heard two different messages from two different ministers. The first was from her ex-husband, who said, "You're worthless. I'm angry at you, and so is God." The second voice was from my grandpa, Dr. Schuller, who said, "You are loved. You're a child of God." She believed the latter, and it gave her the power she needed to escape a violent husband. She really believed God had more for her life than she was currently experiencing, and that belief made all the difference. She was given a personal creed—"God loves you and so do I"—and it empowered her to start a new life.

She explained to me that when she heard Robert Schuller was in town and was down at the Hyatt Regency Hotel, she asked her beloved husband, Israel, to find him and bring him up here so she could tell him how much his words about God's love had changed her life. Unfortunately for her, she got me instead of my grandpa, but she was just as happy to share her story with me. And I'm glad she did. Through her words, I gained a new passion for the message of God's love and dignity for people. I realized then how much *Hour of Power* was touching lives in dramatic ways. I became a believer in TV ministry that evening.

I realized the power of telling someone, simply and without apology, "God loves you." That creed—"God loves you and so do I"—influenced my creed in a big way. I grasped the power of assuring God's love to those who are suffering. I learned the first purpose of every church is to ascribe dignity to lost and broken people. That's what Jesus did. And as a student of Jesus Christ, my task was to be a living reminder of God's love to hurting people.

Years later I remember talking to my grandpa in his office about why he spoke about God's love so much. He favored both architecture and psychology, and this time he gave me a psychological response: "Freud believed the greatest human need is pleasure. Adler believed the greatest human need is power. And Frankl believed the greatest human need is meaning. But I say the greatest human need is dignity." That day in his tower office, I got the words to describe why I got up in the morning: to give, teach, and ascribe dignity and belonging to everyone—to teach people their identity as the beloved.

Dignity means, to a degree, that you should respect everyone. Dignity means viewing people through the lens of the beloved, not the lens of resentment or judgment. It means striving to understand the story and the brokenness of people before rejecting them. It means looking at those who are hurting and believing in them. It says, "You belong before you believe." It repeats the hopeful words of St. Augustine: "There's no saint without a past, and no sinner without a future."

Living in our identity as the beloved is the gateway to a life full of energy because it helps us endure feelings of embarrassment, shame, and rejection. It gives us the inner strength to be vulnerable and share our weaknesses with the people we love. Do you ever feel like your friendships, marriage, family, and work colleagues are draining you? Walking in the dignity of the beloved will free you to make the appropriate steps to turn those relationships into your greatest source of joy.

The Opposite of Dignity Is Shame

After years of ministry serving thousands of hurting people, I've seen how shame leads to death and grace leads to life. Without a doubt, feelings of shame lead to more mistakes, hurtful behavior, addiction, and pretending. Those setbacks and mistakes then intensify the shame that was already present and cause people to feel more worthless and isolated.

Grace, however, causes people to be more trusting. It's healing and allows people to show what's really hurting them.

My friend Matt[1] has talked about what it was like being addicted to crystal meth. He came from a loving Christian home but sometime in high school got involved with the wrong group of friends. These friends introduced him to drugs, and by the middle of college he was totally hooked. He lost everything and was hurting himself and others. This caused him to feel incredible shame, isolating him even more from the thing he needed most: deep connection with friends and family. These feelings of unworthiness became a major emotional trigger for him that elevated his desire for more drugs. He was caught in the cycle of addiction.

Years later he was mentored out of his addiction. He was taught to be vulnerable, to live at peace with his mistakes and his shortcomings. Most important, he got involved with a college church group who accepted him as an addict and loved him through the process. They invited him to be a part of revival nights, where he would enter into prayer and worship for hours. It was these loving, vulnerable connections and a newfound relationship with Jesus that helped my friend overcome shame and reconcile with his friends and family, ultimately beating his addiction. He is now a loving husband and father of three.

Though most people have not been caught in the grip of drug addiction, most of us have a "substance." By that I mean that we all have good things we make bad by using them to escape from our feelings of unworthiness and emptiness. The same addiction cycle can be found in workaholism, compulsive shopping, overeating, or just lethargically napping and watching TV. We see these behaviors aren't good for us. We then feel shame about the results of these behaviors. We beat ourselves up, which triggers the need for more work, shopping, food, naps, TV, or whatever.

God wants to break your need for an escape and give you the life you've always wanted through being the beloved. To have true life we must rid our lives of shame.

Jesus = Anti-Shame

Jesus reveals to us what God is like. Jesus was always carelessly abandoning his own reputation by loving and celebrating people who were societal outcasts. In his day reputation was everything, yet he did things that could harm his reputation. He ate with all the dregs of society, such as tax collectors, Samaritans, and lepers. He ate with business cheats who openly swindled people out of their money, like Zacchaeus. Once he allowed a prostitute to wipe expensive perfume on his feet while weeping. Jesus just didn't care about appearances.

This kind of ministry was radical.

You see, Jesus was a rabbi, and this was not the typical behavior of a rabbi. After all, rabbis were the most respected people in their community. They were moral paragons. Everywhere they went they were honored. People would ask them to rule over legal disagreements. They were always given the best table at community events. They were ribbon cutters, the cream of the crop, and frankly, they didn't like to associate with those who might tarnish their reputation.

Every young boy dreamed of being a rabbi. In order to become one, however, you had to be mentored by another, usually older and established, rabbi. You couldn't just enroll in rabbi school. To begin the journey of ordination, a teenage boy who thought he might have what it takes would go to a rabbi and ask to become his disciple, or protégé. A disciple was more than a student; a disciple was someone who was going to teach Torah and live Torah exactly as the older rabbi did, someone who was supposed to be almost a clone of the mentor.

Most of the time the rabbis would reject these boys because, for the most part, rabbis were really mostly interested in their own social standing. They were "established" for good reason, after all. They only wanted the best of the best—the brightest, holiest, and most disciplined of students. They wanted the Harvard-level disciples because it would make them look good.

Rabbi Jesus was different (and this point is so important). He called the nonreligious, spiritually bankrupt people to be his disciples. He invited poor people, sick people, prostitutes, and fishermen to follow him. This was a huge deal—shocking—and were he not a miracle worker and brilliant teacher, he probably would have lost his position in society for meddling with such "lowlifes."

My favorite example of this is the calling of Saint Matthew. He wasn't a saint at the time. He was a sinful tax collector. If rabbis were the most respected people, tax collectors were the most hated. They were generally considered thieves, and for good reason. Picture the Sheriff of Nottingham in Disney's *Robin Hood* going around taking every last bit of money from the poor, widowed, and disabled. These bullies were hired by the occupying Roman Empire to tax their own people, the Jews. They took whatever they wanted. They didn't have to disclose what percentage of the tax was for Rome and what percentage was for them personally. It was totally arbitrary and, even worse, secret. Tax collectors were loathed. They were seen as turncoats—Jews who sided with the occupying Roman Empire. They were outsiders hated and reviled for their lack of ethics and patriotism.

In Matthew's gospel he gave his own explanation of how he, a tax collector, became a follower of Rabbi Jesus. Early in the story he gave an account of the Sermon on the Mount. Jesus, while standing on a floral hill by the Sea of Galilee on a warm day, looked at everyone with compassion. Those in attendance were everyday people, many of them poor, many of them not religious. It's likely many came because they needed medical attention and didn't know where to turn.

He looked at them and said, "You are the salt of the earth . . . You are the light of the world" (Matt. 5:13, 14). Notice he didn't say, "*Become* salt and light." He proclaimed it over them: "You *are!*"

This is the subtext of this gospel: Matthew was there on that hill, one of the many spectators hearing Jesus' words. He was standing in that crowd thinking, *Not me. There's no way a ragamuffin tax collector like me is salt and light. Jesus doesn't know what I've done.* It's as though he was secretly hoping he could have a different life than the one he got: a do-over, a new chance to be salt and light, to have an existence of true meaning and significance, to help people. I wonder, did he go home sad?

Now let me pause again to explain something. Back then most men did what their dad did for a living. It is likely Matthew's father, grandfather, and great-grandfather were also tax collectors. Think about that: going back for generations, all the men in Matthew's family worked a job that was considered immoral. Matthew's family never *belonged*. Every religious community had rejected these tax collectors from having any part of worship or Jewish life.

Picture this: Matthew was sitting there at his booth, counting his ill-gotten money, and Jesus offered him the incredible honor of becoming an apprentice, to train to become a rabbi. It's crazy. I imagine at first Matthew must have thought Jesus was mocking him. But when he realized, *He's serious*, it's as though you could hear the sound of his table being knocked over, coins chiming everywhere as they carelessly hit the ground, and Matthew practically hollering, "Yes! I will follow you."

Everyone watching was shocked. *Did Jesus just call a tax collector to apprenticeship?* Even more scandalous, Jesus then joined Matthew and his sinner friends at the table, another major cultural bombshell. They were likely a rogue group composed of other tax collectors, prostitutes, and various riffraff you're not likely to see in church. And Jesus just sat there and ate dinner and drank wine with them. You didn't do that if you were a rabbi. Rabbis didn't eat with sinners.

Everyone was confused.

In his day, to eat with someone was to call him or her your equal. For example, kings or dignitaries would eat in elevated or separated positions, or eat at different times altogether, to highlight their separateness from their court and servants. You only ate with people of your equal societal status.

Not Jesus. He ate with everybody.

I imagine this embarrassed his other disciples. "Rabbi, don't you know who this man is?" or "Don't you know who this woman is?" they might have asked.

Here's the moral of the story (and you can't miss this): Jesus ascribed dignity to people *before* fixing them. He loved them not as they should've been but just as they were. He called them *beloved*. Even though they were mess-ups, he invited them to belong. Yes, he challenged them to be better, but first he gave them dignity and a listening ear. He gave them back their humanity. For Jesus, it was first dignity then discipleship.

In a religious world that said, "First you behave, then you belong," Jesus turned it upside down by saying, "First you belong, and then you'll behave."

You belong to Jesus. Maybe you aren't religious, or maybe you walked away from the faith a long time ago. Maybe you have something in your life that is secret, that's embarrassing, and you think if anyone knew about it, no one would see you the same. Perhaps you've already been embarrassed, and now people are holding your past against you. Do you wonder if God is angry with you or has abandoned you altogether? The Scriptures assure us: nothing can separate us from the love of God (see Rom. 8:38–39). He wants only the best for you and is cheering you on to victory. He loves calling misfits and mess-ups to be light and salt.

God's Love Is the Antidote to Shame

If you want to be full of God's energy, you have to find your home in God's love. I've learned that when I lose sight of his love for me, I lose my power to say no to others. I find myself people pleasing, or worse, becoming angry or passive-aggressive. When I lose sight of God's love for me, I feel compelled to prove myself to others. I buy things I don't need. I feel embittered when my work isn't recognized or applauded. All of these behaviors come from a place of wanting to matter and belong. So when I wake up in the morning relaxed, knowing I'm loved by God, many of these bad emotions lose their power over my life.

It's not like we don't know the difference between right and wrong. It's not like we don't understand the concept of working hard to achieve our goals and dreams. The problem is we lack the force to do so because we're busy trying to prove ourselves to others. Shame—that feeling of "I'm not good enough"—keeps creeping its way into our hearts and, like a leech, sucking all the energy and joy from our lives.

God's love is the antidote.

Acclaimed researcher and psychologist Brené Brown reflected, "Most everyone knows how to eat healthy . . . make good choices with our money . . . care for our emotional needs [but] we are the most obese, medicated, addicted, and in-debt Americans ever." Why? Because we don't talk about the greatest thing that gets in the way of doing what's best for ourselves. We don't talk about shame. We "hustle for worthiness" instead of living with a sense of belonging.[2]

God sent his son Jesus to remove not only your sin, but also your feelings of shame and unworthiness. The cross is a reflection of the vastness of God's love for you. You were worth it. You may not think so, but God does. He never does anything that isn't worth doing; you were worth living and dying for. He loves you as much as he loves his son, Jesus Christ. God sees you as I saw my daughter rocking her to sleep many years ago. He'd do anything for you.

Your Personal Creed

We need to get to a place where we can let go and begin to let others see us. We have to train away from our usual behaviors of withdrawing and pretending. We can't simply try harder. We need a process, a method to allow the knowledge "I am loved by God" to go from our head to our hearts.

Developing a personal creed did that for me. I based it partly on a sermon from Henri Nouwen and then on some of the writings of my friend and brief mentor Dallas Willard. I added a little more to it, and after I'd written the Creed of the Beloved, I memorized it and said it multiple times every day. Eventually, it became my prayer.

I was astonished to see how, above any other spiritual discipline I employed, this creed based on Scripture utterly changed my energy level, my feelings of joy, and my outlook on life. After saying it several times a day for a few weeks, my relationship with God reached an incredible new depth. I was living with boundaries. I was opening up more with my wife and friends. Other people started noticing a difference as well. I could see how shame, chronic guilt, and a sense of unworthiness had pervaded my life. I could see how it was getting in the way of my relationship with God and the people I love.

The irony: the more I reinforced and meditated on the idea that "I'm not what I do, what I have, or what people say about me," the better these things went in my life. I was more moral. I acted decently toward people. I was less irritable and had tons of energy, out of nowhere. God was blessing me. And I noticed people had a better opinion of me.

This creed taught me that by letting go, you receive. By being more vulnerable, you become stronger. By not being so busy, you become more productive.

It meant so much to me that after about a year of praying it, I shared it. I did a message series called, "Life of the Beloved." The original plan for our church was to use the creed for the duration of the ten-week series so people could memorize it and use it for themselves. I figured after that time we would move on to something else.

We didn't.

The results were amazing. This biblical creed gave people something in fresh language to use every day in their prayer time. And the word that was most commonly used to describe how it helped was *energy*.

I was surprised. People were experiencing joy and freedom because they were finally understanding and training themselves for a life of grace. Instead of being motivated by guilt, they were totally filled with joy, fresh vision, and a renewed sense of calling. It was so powerful we kept the creed as a part of our regular worship service.

Now, through *Hour of Power*, this has become the personal creed of literally tens of thousands of people and has transformed hearts and lives around the world. We've received so many letters from people who also claimed this prayer changed everything. People have sent us lots of odds-and-ends crafts with the creed on it, such as pillows, watercolor paintings, and sketches from children, all because something so small has changed their lives.

It will change yours too.

I want to encourage you to memorize this creed and say it every day as you read this book. Let this book be a journey into the heart of God. I pray that as you read, you will realize your value in God's world. I promise, if these words can sink into your heart and mind, your life will take a new direction.

If you are already using this creed in your prayer time, this book will help you go deeper into understanding why it's helping so much. No matter who you are, this book is going to get at the heart of how your identity is the source of most of your spiritual and emotional energy. You will finish this book with the tools you need to have way more vigor and joy in life. It's all based on the Bible, and I promise you'll never be the same.

CREED OF THE BELOVED

I'm not what I do.
I'm not what I have.
I'm not what people say about me.
I am the beloved of God. It's who I am. No one can take it from me.
I don't have to worry.
I don't have to hurry.
I can trust my friend Jesus and share his love with the world.

YOU MATTER TO OTHERS
AND THEY MATTER TO YOU

If you want to go quickly, travel alone. If you
want to go far, travel with friends.
—African Proverb

Abide in me and you will bear fruit . . . This
is my command: love one another.
—Jesus (John 15)

Everyone needs and deserves dignity. It is the foundation for a life full of energy. It paves the way for the deepest human need to be met.

The greatest human need is to connect profoundly with others, to have rich, meaningful relationships. When you connect with your friends and family—when they see you deeply, know you well, and, despite your flaws, love you anyway—you have the foundation for true emotional health. As these relationships grow and develop, they will be the source of most of your energy, compelling your work to be more productive and fulfilling. In other words, it's all about friends and family. That's where your emotional strength comes from.

When we find our identity in our vocation or in our morals, our relationships with others become poisoned, as does our relationship with God. They develop into things such as religiosity and workaholism. These don't keep us from having friends and family, but they do keep us from having a great connection with them. The dread of abandonment is the greatest looming human fear, and when the possibility of being embarrassed, rejected, or dumped appears, we hurry to do something—anything—to keep that from happening. Therefore, because of the many pains of rejection in life, we continue to manufacture relationships that aren't really life giving. They may feel safe, but in the end, they're not. The lack of intimacy slowly eats away like termites eat away at a house. Everything may look good, but over time things become brittle and you wonder what went wrong.

The opposite happens when you connect deeply with others. As you do, you become more emotionally alive. You have more joy. Your work has meaning because it's done with others.

This was certainly true in my life. As I became more emotionally alive and connected to others, I found meaning in everything. Fixing and developing my first house wasn't about me; it was about our family. As I grew emotionally with God and others, the ministry I was doing—which before had often felt forced and exhausting—began giving me new life. I started including my wife, Hannah, more, both in worship and behind the scenes and realized this whole time I had been missing out on something big. First, I was missing out on the many gifts and insights Hannah brought to the table, and in giving her a sense of belonging in the ministry. But second, it was something we could do together, like any other project. It became something we could talk and dream about together when we were home praying. It wasn't about me anymore. It was about us.

My Testimony

The last fifteen years of my life have been a long process of coming awake emotionally. I didn't realize it, but much of my life I was totally numb. With the many challenges I faced as a kid, I learned that being tough was a great way to avoid being hurt. This would come out through fighting, sarcastic humor, or checking out altogether into things like television and hobbies.

I never cried. I cried so little that I even noticed it and wondered what was wrong with me. It wasn't that I was strong enough to keep from crying, but rather that I had no feelings at all that would make me want to cry. The most startling experience was how I reacted when my grandpa Pursley from my mother's side of the family was diagnosed with colon cancer. We were very close. He would hang out with me every week and always take me to get ice cream. He taught me Spanish and was always my biggest encourager.

As he was going in for a major surgery, we all knew there was a chance he wouldn't come out. Though I had thoughts of concern, I didn't have the same emotional response everyone else was having. It was so obvious my mom very kindly brought it up to me: "Bobby, you know your grandpa might not make it, right?" I didn't know how to respond. I wondered what was wrong with me. (He made it, by the way, and is still alive and kicking today at ninety years old.)

Even into adulthood, this emotional numbness was something of an issue, though I didn't know it at the time. I had loads of friends, was doing well, and was happily married. Yet even in my marriage I would get hints from Hannah that she needed more from me. Often this confused me and would even make me feel frustrated. As a peacemaker, Hannah would back off and not press the issue, but she desperately needed a deeper connection with me. Everyone did. My friends and family all felt that at some level they were not getting the real me.

Eventually I met my dear friend Bill Gaultiere. He was an Oral Roberts University grad like me, but was about twenty years older. He had an amazing intellect and a sweet soul, and the both of us hit it off. He often invited me to pray with him and to go on walks with him. At first we had very casual conversations about topics like the White Sox. But after we developed a real friendship, Bill started digging into my soul. He helped me piece together a lot of my own story and showed me how to be vulnerable—not only with him, but with Hannah and the other important people in my life. He taught me that I needed empathy and taught me to share my suffering with the people who love me.

Three or four years went by before I realized I was getting free therapy. You see, Bill is a clinical psychologist; he has a PhD and is a renowned writer and thinker in the realm of Christian psychology. More than that, he was mentored by one of my favorite Christian thinkers and writers: Dallas Willard.

Bill had this amazing ability to weave his biblical knowledge and his education into a perfect fit for me. He showed me that I had walled people off from the things I was embarrassed by. I realized I had blocked out a lot of my past that was too painful to think or talk about. I recognized the strong urge to withdraw into entertainment or work when life became too painful. Believe it or not, I had an actual addiction to chess. (I know I sound like a huge nerd right now, but the addiction was real.) But most of all, I had trained myself to not feel, to be emotionally numb. I couldn't help it.

Bill gave me the tools to let my guard down and start letting people in. This changed everything in my life. The tipping point came when I was about twenty-eight. This was when I realized more than any other time in my journey how powerful the unconscious life is.

Hannah and I were driving home late one night from a social gathering. We were talking about this and that, as any couple would. We started telling stories about when we were kids and the funny stuff we did. I began to tell her a story that I thought was very funny. It was about some very clumsy thing I did while visiting with a member of my extended family, someone I was very close to. That clumsy thing was the funny part. The not so funny part was that after I did it, this person dismissed me and yelled, "Get out of here, you s***head!"

Even though I'd been laughing as I told Hannah the story, when I got to that point, everything changed. Mid-sentence my whole countenance went from laughing to grim. I couldn't even say the word. I just locked up. My eyes got watery, and I started weeping. I've never cried so hard in my life. The whole way home, with Hannah patting my back saying, "It's okay," I struggled to gain my composure. Walking into the house, I finally got it together and held it for about five minutes. But as soon as she went to brush her teeth, I went into the tool shed behind the house and wept even more.

It was one of the most bizarre experiences of my life. Consciously I'd thought the story was very funny. But when I began to tell it out loud, the unconscious part of my mind, which had been grieving over it since I was a child, erupted. The latter emotion totally overcame the former. I realized that on the surface I could act tough, confident, and dignified, but somewhere deep inside was the hidden feeling I was an unwanted piece of s***.

I wept. I'd needed this. More than any other experience in my life, I realized that night there was a lot under the surface I was completely unaware of. That year, I stepped into a new experience with God and people that has been the greatest source of energy and joy in my life. It's almost like when you wake up in the morning and your arm is completely numb. It takes a while to come back. You first feel it tingling, then you feel pain, then you get your strength back. That's what happened to me emotionally. I continue on this journey today and still have a lot of work to do. But more than anything, I realize this is what it's all about: connecting deeply with others and with God.

That weeping experience wasn't just good for me. It was good for Hannah. I remember when Hannah and I were dating, it was a constant struggle for her to feel that I loved her. I assure you, I very much did love her, was mad about her, would buy her gifts, take her to nice dinners, say romantic things to her. And yet, something was missing. The thing she was missing, I only realized later, was my vulnerability. I was present but could be cold somehow, unfeeling. At the time I actually was cold, not really emotionally alive.

Weeping in front of her that first time, I was so embarrassed. I kept apologizing.

"No! It's okay," she said over and over, almost hollering. She couldn't believe it. I was finally opening up, trusting her to see a very deep wound. This is what she'd needed from me most: my vulnerable, true self and my trust. I realized she wouldn't reject or take advantage of me if I stopped being a stoic know-it-all once in a while. That was part of a long journey where we learned about not bottling our stresses, losses, and disappointments. Instead, being wholeheartedly true, honest, and vulnerable paved the way for us to bond in deeper ways, giving us both more energy and life.

Reach Out to Others. Be Vulnerable.

Being vulnerable with someone you love is one of the best ways to make him or her feel valued, trusted, and even safe. When you share your secret stuff with people, they know they will be less likely to be judged or abandoned when they share with you. We think being open and honest about our sins, regrets, doubts, fears, and stresses will push people away. Sometimes it does, but almost always it draws people closer. This is because when you are vulnerable, you are saying, "I trust you. I like you. I'm not judging you. I want you to see me." When you are vulnerable, others will more likely be honest and feel safe around you. You'll be easier to talk to because it's easier to dialog with sinners than saints. It's easier to be honest with a drunk than with a pastor. The only people who are truly growing in their inner lives are those who have learned to let go and trust their lives to God and learned to be at peace with their imperfections.

Have you ever—in spite of having lots of friends or a big family—felt lonely, even isolated? Have you thought to yourself, *Why do I feel this way? I'm completely surrounded by my people, people who love me.* So many of us have this sense there's something missing—something deep and indescribable. We look for ways to ignore this void, to go on, to just endure.

That nagging feeling is loneliness, and it's driving all the negative things we do. This is because our greatest need is to connect deeply with others. The need isn't to merely have a spouse, a girlfriend or boyfriend, or lots of friends or people in your life. Many of us have many relationships and yet feel a sense of emptiness and loneliness even though we are not alone. Hannah felt that way with me.

Rather, we need more than people. We need the people we love to see us deeply, to accept us where we are with all our flaws. We need to be trusted enough so that others allow us to see their imperfections as well. When the soul is rooted in the love of God, it becomes safe to reach out to others while being truly you. If you experience rejection or betrayal, you simply fall back on the safety net that is the person of Jesus Christ, who says:

> You're not what you do,
> you're not what you have,
> and you're not what people say about you.
> You are my beloved.

So much of life is about energy—about having what it takes to keep going. And not only to keep going, but to go on with joy, with real vibrancy. Life is all about waking up ready to take on another day because we are energized and excited about its possibilities. This joy belongs to those who for whatever reason have decided that being vulnerable and bonding deeply with others is the most important thing. Seeing others deeply and being seen deeply by others is what it's all about.

The more we unconsciously feel lonely, isolated, and unfulfilled, the more tempted we are to withdraw into our old habits, to disappear into eating, watching TV, or going back to whatever old routine helped us escape.

But when we have real, deep love for our dear friends, our colleagues, our spouse, or our kids, life has what I refer to as *verve*. The dictionary defines *verve* as "vigor" or "enthusiasm." It's what happens when we live believing we are the beloved of God. When we know that God loves us unconditionally, it releases an abundant flow of his energy in us.

Have you ever had a gripping conversation with an old friend—maybe by the fire, maybe with a cup of coffee—and though it was hours long, it seemed to go by quickly? You went to bed in the early hours of the morning, tired because it was late, but energized because of the good time you had. If you are married, you might even remember those kinds of conversations with your spouse when he or she was still just your boyfriend or girlfriend. That kind of amazing conversation is called *flow* and it's one of the best things in the world. It yields incredible energy over a long period of time. It fills the tank.

Maybe you've had the opposite experience. You're with someone you love, but you can't seem to get past talking about the mundane "How's the weather" kind of talk. It's exhausting. We avoid people who have too many conversations like that with us. This is because these types of conversations fall flat of our expectations. As we desire to connect deeply with others, shallow conversations feel like a waste of time and drain the tank completely. They might even trigger the need to escape.

I remember a time when our old small group broke the boring dialogue that often accompanies a planned gathering and began to flow in a deep, bonding conversation. There were about ten of us, sitting by the fire in a dimly lit room with all kinds of snacks. Someone asked, "What is the number one thing someone could say or do that would offend you?" I was surprised by not only how different the responses were, but how it revealed some of our deepest wounds.

One of the girls shared that if someone implied or outright said, "We don't want your opinion," it would break her heart. She cried as she told us this about herself. Incidentally, three of our small-group members were siblings: two guys and a girl. They all three had the same response: the most offensive person was someone who was condescending and said, "Oh, you don't understand the real world," or who belittled them by saying, "That's so cute." Apparently their dad did this often to all three of them.

This conversation quickly led to revealing some of our deepest wounds we didn't know were still affecting our character and choices. Mine was and still is being called *stupid*.

More important, this level of vulnerability brought our group to a whole new level of trust and joy. We were flowing. We were filling up our tank and setting up our whole week and perhaps month to be full of joy and energy.

As noted earlier, shame is the greatest thing that gets in the way of this all-encompassing deep need. Shame looks like hiding—constantly managing the way people see you. It says, "If people knew *this* about me, they would reject me, avoid me, and be embarrassed to be seen with me." Shame takes the form of a rigid worldview: everything in black and white, an absolute certainty of how things are, with little room for other opinions. For instance, have you ever known someone who is so fierce about their political or religious views, he or she is mean to anyone who disagrees with them? If so, you're looking at someone who struggles with shame and feels unworthy of love and belonging.

In this way, shame becomes sin. That sin then causes people to feel more shame and become even more isolated from others.

God sees you—everything in your past and in your heart—and dares you to believe he loves you. People love you too. In fact, when you yield the idea that you can control outcomes, your public reputation, or life in general, then and only then do you receive freedom. This is called *grace*.

This is why believing the Creed of the Beloved is so important. It causes God's grace and love to move from something we talk about in church to being something that abides deep in our soul. This spiritual discipline challenges us to examine our fears and behaviors against the backdrop of God's love.

If you think, *They will never take me back because of what I did*, the creed would say, "Why not try? You're not what you do." If you feel like, *I don't fit in here. I don't drive the nice cars they drive. I don't have a degree. I don't have kids*, God says to you, "You're not what you have. Reach out to them. You are more wanted than you think."

You remember the nasty things people said about you in the past? Oftentimes your behavior shows they were right. God says over you, "You're not who others say you are. You're my beloved. Live from that place and reach out to others. You need them, and they need you."

The Creed of the Beloved trains us to abandon all the fake stuff in our lives and simply find a home in our identity as the beloved. It gives us the resilience to bounce back after being rejected or embarrassed. Saying it in a spirit of prayer and allowing it to sink deeply into our hearts can be the key that allows us to take big risks in going deeper with others.

The best way to have more emotional and spiritual energy is to connect deeply with others, to believe you are worthy of that belonging and connection, to believe you have something to offer, and to stop giving all your time to things that don't matter. Dying people don't think about their accomplishments; they think about their relationships. We'll be thinking about those whom we love and who love us. That's really all that matters, and everything in life should be built around that. So don't be afraid to reach out to others.

Abide in the Vine of God's Love

In John 15 Jesus taught his disciples that if they wanted to bear fruit, they needed to abide in him. This word *abide* in Greek is *meno*. Jesus used it over and over in this passage. He said if you abide, or *meno*, in him, you will bear fruit. By being firmly rooted in him you will have the strength to reach out and love others. In other words, if you want to love others and be loved by others, you need the security of knowing you are ultimately safe in God's love. We love because he first loved us. Finding your identity in being the beloved is the only way you will find safety in reaching out to others.

We don't have a word exactly like *meno* in English. *Abide* is the best we can do. The word *meno* is all about being at home. It's like this: Have you ever been in the mountains, hiking or sledding in the snow, and come home, and everything on your body is cold and wet? Maybe it got really cold—colder than it already was—and you had this sense of urgency to just get back to the cabin. The wind and snow were starting to pick up, and all of a sudden you felt unsettled. You started heading back in the general direction of the cabin, but you weren't quite sure . . .

Then, just as you crested the top of the hill, you saw in the long, white distance a cabin with plumes of smoke puffing diagonally from the chimney. Home.

Coming back into the cabin there was a fire in the fireplace. It was warm and safe, and though you could see a blizzard outside, you just watched its beauty safely behind a frosty glass pane. You took off your outer jacket and stomped off the snow from your boots. Someone had just made some hot chocolate, and it was waiting for you. You peeled your wet socks off your feet. They went on the brick in front of the fire, and you put your feet up to warm them and were comfy. You were home.

That feeling is *meno* or *abide*. It's the place where you are safest, feel most comfortable, and belong. It's a shelter from the bad weather outside. It's home.

Jesus teaches us that when our soul abides in God, we are safe to reach out to others. Some may reject us or hurt us, but in the end we know we are safe because our soul always has a cabin to come home to. We can be open and honest about who we are and endure any rejection that might come.

As we reach out to others and begin bonding and flowing, we get a deeper sense that we have a place in the world. We believe more deeply in God's love and feel it through other people. This feeling is deeply gratifying and has the power to break our depression, addiction, workaholism, and feelings of boredom. It's so powerful. When this happens, the cycle of shame, sin, and isolation begins to go the other way. By being vulnerable and reaching out to others, we bond. This bonding in turn gives us emotional energy and joy, driving us to further altruism and a deeper sense of dignity. We feel even safer to reach out and go deeper. Life is changed.

I can't emphasize enough how important this is. Jesus changed the lives of his disciples by going deep with them over three years of ministry. This relationship was maintained after his death, resurrection, and ascension through meals and gatherings that would eventually become the church. People were worshiping, working, living, and giving in deep soul-friendships. God's love was felt through other people.

That continues today. You can't grow into a happy and whole student of Jesus if you are not giving priority to your relationships.

Believe You Are Wanted

Do you think and feel you are wanted just as you are and not as you should be? Do you believe people really long to spend time with you? If you feel fear or shame, let go of it. You are wanted by the people who love you.

Sometimes we won't share an opinion or tell someone we are angry because we are afraid of pushing him or her away. That fear comes from a place of shame. It's a way of saying, "My opinion is not important enough to hurt his feelings," or "I'll just make her angry again." This self-talk cuts us off from the person we're afraid of offending and further reinforces our feelings of unworthiness.

When anger is bottled up, it can turn into passive-aggressive behavior. Others feel like they have to read our minds because we won't be honest with them, and when they don't read our minds the right way, we blow up. Sometimes this eruption can be about something completely unrelated to the thing we're actually frustrated about, which makes it even more confusing for our friend or family member.

You can and should be vulnerable about your fear and anger. Anger can be rooted in the fact you are scared—scared your spouse doesn't want you, scared you're going to be stuck with more responsibility than you signed up for, or scared you won't be understood—so you lash out. Sometimes a feeling of fear comes across as anger or even rage. Believe you are wanted so that you can relax. You don't need to lash out. You can be honest and real with the people you love without being mean. They need to really know who you are, and you need to be truly seen.

You are wanted. You are wanted when you are sick. You are wanted when you are unemployed. You are wanted when you are addicted. You are wanted when you are angry. You are wanted when you feel depressed and too tired. You are wanted when you are misunderstood. Your friends and family want you just as you are and not as you should be.

Gratitude Is the Currency of Love

For most of us the problem isn't that we lack relationships; it's that we lack deep and vulnerable relationships. We are too afraid to reach out. Often, our attempts to go deeper fall flat or feel awkward. We backpedal with a couple of jokes and give up on the idea altogether.

Here I want to offer you a very scary challenge, but one that will reap incredible benefits in your personal life. Psychologist and author Martin Seligman spent much of his career studying the science of happiness and found what many other researchers found: the greatest way to increase your happiness is through regular practices of gratitude. He took that notion a step further by connecting it to going deeper with the people we love.

He would challenge his students to write a "gratitude letter" to an important person in their lives. They were not only to write the letter to that person, but also read it aloud to them and give them the letter after reading it. They weren't allowed to make jokes, and they weren't allowed to tell the person beforehand what they were doing. They simply had to visit with them and spontaneously read the letter.

After doing this over the years and collecting the data, Seligman found that these "gratitude visits" greatly increased the happiness of both the writer and the listener for more than a month. Did you catch that? One small act of gratitude and deep connection filled the tank for a whole month.[1]

I want to encourage you to write a letter for someone—right now. Don't overthink it, and don't make it too long. Don't put any jokes in it. Make the whole thing real and from the heart. Think of that special person and write a short message to him or her. It doesn't need to be Shakespeare. Just shoot for a paragraph or so. If it goes longer, fine. But just do your best to put down a few sentences. If it's someone living with you, go over and read it to them right after you finish writing it. If it's someone else, schedule a time for coffee or something similar, and read the letter aloud. Don't give an explanation. Just pull it out and start reading. I guarantee this small act will propel your friendship or relationship to a new level of trust, joy, and energy.

If you do this and want to share your story with me, I want to hear it. You can write to me at the address below and it will land squarely on my desk:

Bobby Schuller
Attn: Gratitude Letter
P.O. Box 100
Garden Grove, CA 92842

The key is to do it now. Otherwise you will say, "I'll do it some other time. Maybe tomorrow," or "I need time to think." Delaying only means you won't do it. Don't have paper? Just write it on the back page of this book and read it to them later. God wants you to have more energy by connecting deeply with others, but you have to do the brave thing and step out in courage.

If you are afraid you might be embarrassed, just say the Creed of the Beloved to yourself and remember:

YOU MATTER TO OTHERS AND THEY MATTER TO YOU

You're not what you do,

You're not what you have,

You're not what other people say about you.

You are the beloved of God.

You don't need to worry. You don't need to hurry.

You can trust your friend Jesus and share his love with the world.

3

YOU'RE NOT WHAT
YOU DO AS A VOCATION

Come to me, all you who are weary and burdened, and I will
give you rest. Take my yoke upon you and learn from me,
for I am gentle and humble in heart, and you will find rest for
your souls. For my yoke is easy and my burden is light.
—Jesus Christ (Matt. 11:28–30)

Work is good for the soul, but only to the point it doesn't take priority over the most important things in your life: your walk with God, your family, and your friends.

My dear friend and executive pastor at *Hour of Power*, Russ Jacobson, has told a story of how he came to learn this personally. In his pursuit of ordination, Russ had to intern as a chaplain at what he called "the Rolls Royce of nursing homes," located here in one of the richest cities in wealthy Orange County. Here the elite of Southern California would come to live out the remainder of their days as they grew older and were unable to care for themselves. He would meet and pray with former hedge-fund managers, attorneys, government officials, and chancellors of major universities.

Too often Russ would hear the same story play over and over. These people who used to have everything in the world now lived in a ten-by-twelve white room with just a TV and a bed. They would tell Russ with regret about their accomplishments. They had neglected their spouses and children for the dream of ultimate success and now wondered, *Where are my family and my friends? Where is God?* Too often, those who used to be the most powerful and influential people in California would die alone because they hadn't recognized the importance of their relationship with God and others.

Because of this experience, Russ left his family's lucrative accounting business to work with the church and make an impact with his life for God. Even more important, he's one of the best dads and husbands I've known. He cares more about family than anything and incidentally is one of the most energetic people I know.

I believe these two things—connecting with God and others and having lots of energy—are related. The energy we get from a deep relationship with God and others is the kind we need to make our work fulfilling. Ironically, the first step for most people is to recognize their own limitations and let go of expectations. It is so important to let go of the idea that you are what you do for a living. You are not what you do morally, and you are not your achievements. You are not a parent, a pastor, a friend, a spouse, or anything else you do; you are a beloved child of God.

> You are not a parent, a pastor, a friend, a spouse, or anything else you do; you are a beloved child of God.

Society imprints a very different message on our minds and hearts, and because of this, everyone's exhausted. People use jobs as the primary way to get to know one another. Anytime you go to a social gathering people will ask you what you do for a living. By knowing you are a stay-at-home mom or a bus driver or a doctor, people instantly make assumptions about who you are. They can't help but leap from your answer to making quick conclusions about your income, your hobbies, and whether you are a winner or loser in life. They also get a better sense of whether you might click as an associate or even a friend.

Ascribing value based on what we do is a deep source of anxiety for most people because it touches on our greatest fear: the fear of abandonment. All of us struggle with this. C. S. Lewis reckoned it to circles. Everyone wants to be included in the circle, and no one wants to be excluded. So when we know that "what we do" will have significant bearing on whether or not we'll be accepted in various circles, we're likely to do more than we should to prove ourselves to others and be "worthy" of their friendship.

As a pastor, I hate getting asked what I do for a living. My guard instantly goes up and I wonder if I can be honest. I think to myself, *Have I said or done something during our brief conversation that was un-pastorly?* When I tell people I'm a pastor, I do get various reactions, but it's usually awkward silence. Some people ask me to pray with them, which is nice, but I instantly feel a sad sense of separation. I'm their pastor now.

I remember once going golfing at this very blue-collar golf course across from the church. It's thirteen dollars at twilight if you carry your own bag, and that always sounds like free to me. It also sounds like free to everyone else and tends to drag out all the other guys like me who can't afford a real golf course. This particular day I got paired up with a really funny guy whom I'll call Gus. Gus was golfing without a shirt, and he chose flip-flops as his golf shoe of choice. He was drunk before we even started and had foul enough language to make a rapper blush. But, for whatever reason, Gus and I really liked each other and were having a terrific time. He was actually very funny.

About halfway through the course, a couple of hours into the game, it was like we were best friends. We were probably at that point where you might exchange numbers with someone so you could "do this again sometime." Then he did it: he asked me what I did for a living. I was so sad. I told him as casually as I could that I was a pastor, and that was it.

He instantly got quiet, awkwardly said a little bit of this and that, and kept his distance the rest of the game.

I can only assume Gus leapt immediately to conclusions about my character and probably felt something like shame or anger that I allowed him to go on with his imperfections without letting him know who I was. For whatever reason, the deeply ingrained narrative of "you are what you do" labeled me a judgmental pastor and Gus a drunk. As it always does, being defined by what we did ruined our day.

It's a constant struggle to say and believe, "I'm not what I do; I'm the beloved of God. I'm not what I do; I'm the righteousness of God in Christ Jesus. I'm not what I do; I'm what Christ did for me." But the struggle must continue if you want to live an energetic life of zeal and power.

You likely put a lot of pressure on yourself to do more than is required of you. It's difficult not to compare yourself to others and think, *I'm not as important, successful, or interesting as they are.* This kind of thinking is death. Let go of trying to be and do everything. Know your limitations. You can't do everything, and God doesn't expect you to.

Once, I was sitting at my desk in my little office at the top of the stairs and saw a Facebook video that—I'm not going to lie—made me tear up a little bit. It was a video about young moms and how they viewed themselves. These moms were asked, "How do you think you're doing as a mom?" Each had a different answer, but all were generally the same: "I'm not good enough." One said she doubted too much, another wished she would listen more, another wanted to be more confident, and nearly all of them said they struggled with patience. The last mom perhaps said the most by simply looking down and giving a big sigh.

Watching the video of the moms clearly showed they were beating themselves up. They were all youngish but seemed completely exhausted, as though their inner dialogue was, *I'm not doing well enough and I need to try harder.*

Next, they showed each of these moms a video of their own kids responding to the same question: "How's your mom doing?" Of course, the kids absolutely adored their moms:

- "My mom is totally awesome."
- "She's fun to snuggle with."
- "She loves me a lot. She's my hero."
- "She's so funny."
- "I love to jump on the trampoline with her. We love to jump high."
- "She's so pretty."
- "We color together and go on dates together."

The last kid, a young adolescent girl, said, "She's like my heart, I guess you could say, 'cause she's that close to me."

I continued to watch as each mom cried and seemed to drop a tremendous weight off their shoulders. They'd felt exhausted, not good enough, insufficient, and impatient and had probably compared themselves to other "perfect" moms. But they received freedom when their children affirmed them and spoke a blessing over them. It was as though they'd had a looming fear of not being enough. Their own children freed them from that burden.

It struck a chord with me. I often feel that way as a dad. I know my wife and many of her friends can feel the same way too.

Beyond parenting, this story touches on a deep societal issue of insufficiency, scarcity, and comparison. We're all tired. We're tired not only because we do so much, but also because we do so much from a place of trying to prove ourselves to others. We compare and try to catch up and then feel shame when we just can't make it happen. We wake up in the middle of the night to go to the bathroom and can't fall back asleep because we think of something we said or did and feel a lingering sense of fear or embarrassment. We say to ourselves, "I'll do more. I'll try harder," all the while wondering where we will find the time or the energy.

Sound familiar?

Take a deep breath and lift up your chin. You do enough and you are enough. You are doing a lot better than you think. You deserve respect for what you've accomplished and for the good decisions you've made. You can relax, and you can stop worrying. No one is perfect, and we all have setbacks. Don't beat yourself up. Start smiling, and know that you are doing great. You are a beloved child of God, and you don't have to prove anything to anyone. You are not what you do.

How did it feel to read that last paragraph? If you didn't reject it, as I'm sure you were tempted to do, it probably felt really good. It felt good because it's what you ultimately need. You need to know that you're already doing plenty, that lots of people are proud of you and love you, and that maybe the best thing you can do is do less.

Society in its own way sends the opposite message: Try harder. Do more. Get with the program. Our adrenaline-driven world is hurried and stressed out. Everyone's exhausted. We have equated busyness and a cluttered calendar with success and non-work and rest with sloth and laziness. We easily find ourselves holding on so tightly to everything that our closed fists become a symbol of our hearts: *Don't give. Keep fighting. Hold on tightly.* We look forward to the end of the day thinking it will be relaxing and enjoyable, but when we get there we can barely muster up enough energy to watch TV. And there on TV we are reminded once again of how far ahead of us so many are.

Time to go to bed. Looks like I'm getting less than seven hours of sleep tonight.

Busyness has become a societal virtue, a status symbol. It's become a sign of importance and of being needed. When we call a friend to ask for something, we usually begin with, "I know you're busy," or "I know this is a crazy time for you. You've got tons going on in your life." These are, oddly, compliments. We're saying, "Your busyness shows you are important and needed. Any time to pencil in a friend?"

Think about the opposite. What if you were to say, "I know you have nothing going on right now," or "I'm sure your calendar is completely open." That's an insult, because a full, cluttered calendar belongs to the important, in-demand person, and the light, relatively empty calendar belongs to the unwanted.

What if that's completely wrong? When we compare ourselves to the world, we will always find ourselves in a place of joyless insufficiency, and we will attempt to supplement that existence with overwork and self-bullying when we can't fit the bill. But what if our work came from a deeper place of vision and joy? What if we worked hard, not to prove ourselves, but because it was life giving, even fun? This is what can happen when we let go of managing our reputations and proving ourselves to others and instead live from a place of deep connection with God and with people.

Living from a Place of Rest and Peace

Letting go of the idea that "I am what I do" is all about priorities. It doesn't mean we should not do anything or that we should be lazy. Yes, there are times when we absolutely have projects or deadlines that put us into overdrive, but this is not the way to live life day to day. If we crowd our schedule to prove we are better at our job or are a better parent or a better Christian, we are manufacturing worthiness and not living from a place of real power.

Life must be rooted in rest and peace. It all begins there. One way this is practiced in the normal Christian life is in the context of work and the Sabbath and how they fit together in the life of a believer.

Sunday is the first day of the week, not the last. That may be a surprise, as Monday at least feels like the first day. Look at your calendar. Sunday is almost always the first one on the left. But we don't go to bed on Saturday thinking, *Well, tomorrow I've got to start my week. I wonder how this one's going to go?* Instead, we pair the last and first days of the week together as a weekend, thinking of those two days as a reward for suffering through the first five.

Many of us work really hard at jobs we don't really love, arriving dog tired at the weekend to receive our "reward" for enduring a week of hell. In other words we spend five days unhappy in the hopes of inheriting two days of joy. But it doesn't work out this way. Typically, when we get to the weekend, we spend a lot of that time watching TV or wandering aimlessly around on the Internet or our phones. Somehow we find ourselves staying busy with random stuff. We don't really feel like it was all we hoped it would be. Many of us joke about how it feels when, on Sunday afternoon, say around two o'clock, we get this looming feeling that we're going to have to go to work or school the next day.

It doesn't have to be that way.

Christianity offers a different idea. Our first day of the week is not Monday, a day of labor. It's Sunday, a day or rest and worship. We gather with our church, where we realign our lives with the Word of God and connect deeply with friends and family. We have music, sermons, and stories, as well as special events such as family-night suppers, chili cookoffs, or hayrides that remind us to let go of work—to let go of the grind and have a day of fun and relaxation that really counts. The week begins from a place of rest and worship so that we can enter our work week with the call of God and live from a place of his power.

Ideally, you want to go to work energized and yet relaxed, living in every moment with openness to God's voice and promptings. The workplace in this respect can become a mission field and take on more meaning than the work itself. One church near my home has a sign for parishioners exiting on Sunday. It says, "Ministry begins now," reminding everyone to make the most of their week, to make every conversation count, to be salt and light to hurting neighbors, friends, and even enemies.

I would just add that one of the best ways to be an example is by working every day relaxed. By being relaxed in our work, we think more. We have a happier and more peaceful vibe, one that is open to comforting others, that is interruptible. In this way many who walk in the rhythms of a restful Sabbath approach their Monday as the second day of the week and see the job at Starbucks or the law firm or at home raising kids as a mission, deeper than the thing itself.

Many churches do not teach Sabbath in this way, but still, it's a reminder of the old-school idea in the Christian faith. Power comes from God and not from us. Success comes from discernment and rest, not from grinding away and trying harder. Working from a place of joy is much more productive than working from a place of "not enough" or "proving myself." Even God rested, and we should too. But true rest means letting go, loosening your grip on life, on your goals, your reputation, and your worries.

Ultimately, beginning your week on Sunday instead of Monday is a way of saying, "It all starts with rest." It's a way of saying, "God, I can't do this on my own. I need a day to be with you and the ones I love. I need a day to remind myself I'm not what I do for a living. I'm not a machine. It's not about being more productive. In the end, my relationship with you and with people is the most important thing." Sunday Sabbath is just one practical way to train yourself to let go of an identity based on what you do.

That's ultimately what God wants from you. He wants you to let go. You can't do everything. You can't be perfect. Be at peace with that, and you will have more freedom to put first things first and second things second. You can work hard and even be ambitious, but in the end you must abandon the outcomes to God. Trust that if things don't go your way, it's okay. That's life. Being at peace with this is the beginning of walking as the beloved and having tons of energy.

The Gift of Winter

Letting go of a false identity rooted in what you do can be a painful process and can feel like a winter in your life. Maybe letting go means working less or quitting your job so you can be with your kids more. Maybe letting go means coming to grips with a divorce or empty nesting. Letting go may mean you can't do as much as you used to or handing off a business to the next generation. Most of the time, these dramatic changes in what we do can be arduous, emotional, and very uncomfortable, even if we feel like it's the right thing.

Though in the long run these kinds of moves will very often give you life, they can also feel depressing. It can feel like you're giving up on life. From an anxious place you may find yourself asking, "What am I going to do now?" It can feel like a spiritual winter. You may get to that place and find yourself asking, "God, why am I here? This isn't fair."

Though winter is painful and uncomfortable, it's natural. We may not love it, but often it's just the thing we need to grow into the next chapter of our story. In this respect, the winters of our lives become a gift. Though they can feel isolating, cold, and difficult, it's sometimes in that very place we are most prepared for the destiny God has laid before us. We stand back and in that restful place can see all the ways we have gone astray from our original vision. We get a sense of strength and resolve that there may be another way forward.

Americans have become summer people. We are builders, makers, and dreamers. We like to see harvest, again and again. Our spiritual leaders are obsessed with numbers and output. Most people in America have at least a small sense of business and the way money works. The desire to be rich is immense. We are perhaps the most industrious nation the world has ever seen. But undergirding our hard-working culture is a deep, spiritual exhaustion—three hundred million people with "means to live but no meaning to live for," as Viktor Frankl, the acclaimed author and psychologist who survived a concentration camp during the Holocaust, said. No doubt we have created the largest economy human history has ever seen, yet people are tired and have a distressing sense that life is passing them by.

We have forgotten that winter is a part of healthy growth. Fruit-bearing plants aren't supposed to always bear fruit. They grow in their season. But that harvest season is connected to the greater cycle of winter rest, spring planting, summer tending, and fall harvesting. Winter must happen.

In this way winter is a gift. When winter comes, the earth rests. Everything stops and nothing grows. When it snows like a soft white blanket over your home, everything seems to be quiet and still. For months, very little happens and everything is cold, as though the whole world is napping. The world needs to rest if it's to keep on spinning. So do you. Sometimes the soul needs to be forced from its summer and harvest time, to move to its next place in God's plan.

Years back, when I was living in Tulsa, Oklahoma, to attend college, I missed Southern California and the luxury of seasons on demand. Tulsa summers can crest over 110 degrees for several days, even at night. That's such a strange thing—going outside at night to 105 temps. Bugs—big ugly bugs—are everywhere. There are astounding lightning storms in the spring and fall. But the winters are the worst.

Once, on an early winter morning, I found my car covered in ice. I would have to de-ice it to drive to school. I started the car early, running the heater on full blast. After half an hour the ice hadn't thawed at all. The wind chill (a term I was previously unfamiliar with in my home of Los Angeles) was well below zero, and I was out there trying my best to get the ice off my windshield with a small plastic scraper. While fruitlessly scraping my windshield, I ever so slightly bumped my frigid knuckle on part of the car. The pain was so nasty it dropped me to my knees. In agony I threw the scraper and yelled, "Why am I here?!"

If you're in a winter of your life, you may be asking God the same question: "Why am I here?" Perhaps you've been unemployed a while or are on leave. Maybe you've been sick a while, you're going through a season of loss, or have lost your path forward. I want you to know you're going to be okay. God's got your back and has a way forward for you. Don't rush the winter. Believe that something good can come from this place of in-between. I know you want to move on to spring, but sometimes that doesn't come until we learn to let go. You don't have to worry about spring coming. It always does.

We fail to see how winter can be a gift because we fail to understand how important rest and reflection are. Rest is the birthplace of vision. Long, extended breaks or vacations become fruitful only at the point where they become boring. Only then and there are we forced to look inward at what nags us. There we can step outside of our story to get a clearer picture. There we can get a fresh dream for our lives. Rest is the place where healing and rejuvenation come from, it's where we most clearly hear from and connect with God and others. It's no wonder resting once a week is one of the Ten Commandments.

The soul is like a tulip. Tulips can't grow in the spring unless they have first been frosted in the winter. You can't get to your destiny by grinding away in summer forever. You need to embrace the winters of your life, along with all your imperfections, all of the things you think make you not enough, and trust that God in his sovereignty and grace will tie up all the loose ends. Surrender. Give it to God and learn to go with his flow. You can trust him in the in-betweens of life.

So do less, that you can become more. Let go of the many things that keep you bound to the drudgery of this world, and turn your heart to heaven. Here are some simple yet difficult things that will move you away from reputation management and into living every day at peace with God and yourself:

Rest on Purpose

You deserve real rest. You deserve the kind of rest that makes you take a deep breath and say, "Wow, that was awesome." I'm not talking about cruising compulsively around the Internet and social media. I'm also not talking about getting a little work done around the house or running errands. Try and think of the times when you feel most alive, relaxed, and fulfilled. For me, taking walks around the bay behind my house always does it. I love going with my wife and slowly talking about the day. A fire and a cup of coffee does it too. Even if it's warm outside, I just turn on the air conditioning and fake myself out. Staring at a crackling fire is so much more relaxing than staring at a screen. You deserve the kind of rest that makes you go to bed with a smile on your face thinking, *This was a good day.*

Not long ago I had the house all to myself for a couple of hours. I was so excited. When you have two little kids, there is nothing like having time alone. For the first half hour or so, I "relaxed" by checking four e-mails that had come later in the day. I read an article about how a bus killed a bunch of people at a Christmas market in Germany. That disturbed me, and I soon found myself checking, without even thinking, all my social media. I went from Instagram to Twitter to Facebook and back to Instagram again. I was in a social-media death spiral. I thought, *I have the whole house to myself. What am I doing?*

I stopped. I had been doing "stuff" during my time alone. It was compulsive and unnecessary and certainly not restful. Leaving my phone by my computer upstairs, I walked slowly downstairs, where I put a nice fire on in the fireplace, poured some expensive tea that had been accidentally sent to our house weeks earlier, sat on the couch, and took a deep breath. It wasn't long before I wanted to go upstairs to check my phone. *What if my whole family dies in a car accident and the police can't get ahold of me because I'm resting?* I stayed. I waited. My shoulders dropped, and the Lord met me there. An hour later my family came through the door all smiles and kisses. It was a good night.

Ruthlessly Eliminate Hurry from Your Life

This idea is so important and central to the Creed of the Beloved, yet we try to prove ourselves through our "doing" in order to please others and find a place in our society. Busyness—the chronic need to have a cluttered life—is most evident in our hurry, the greatest sign that we are weak and afraid.

Once, my dear friend and mentor Bill was walking with Dallas Willard. Dallas asked Bill, "If you were to give one word to describe Jesus, what would it be?"

Bill thought about how to answer the simple question. Jesus was *loving. Powerful. Wise.* So many things. Struggling under pressure to find an answer, he finally retorted, "What one word would you give?"

Dallas said, "Jesus was *relaxed*."

I think about this story all the time because it's a definite outlier. Of all words why would one of my favorite heroes, the one and only Dallas Willard, call Jesus relaxed?

I couldn't deny the word fit. Think about it: he was never in a hurry. People constantly needed him, and yet he was slow from point A to point B. He was interruptible, yet was able to say no. He was silent when accused, often went to lonely places to pray, and took a nap in a storm. He was relaxed and never in a hurry. It's because he's so powerful. A relaxed posture is the ultimate sign of power.

Being busy is not a sign of strength but a sign of weakness. Those who live relaxed seem somehow destined to wear a crown. They appear larger than life and undeterred by the alarms of living. Those unhurried souls who infrequently cross our paths seem the master of their destiny and indeed the masters of time itself.

Hurrying doesn't make you faster. It makes you clumsy. But an unhurried, restful person at least appears to be in control, wise, and strong.

Leave Gaps and Arrive Early

We don't feel like there's a lot of time; it's a rare resource, and we don't want to waste it. Most of the time I wake up with not enough sleep. The rest of the day I do my best to shave as much time as possible from this and that to make more of the little time I have. I'm living this day from a place of scarcity and a feeling of not having enough. So when I have an appointment at two o'clock I intend to get there at exactly two o'clock. Not one fifty-eight but two. Then something happens. There's traffic, an accident, or I just didn't time it right, and I have to send an illegal text while driving that I'm going to be late.

You don't need to live this way. You are the beloved. You deserve to live a life with gaps, a life where you can drive slowly in the right lane with plenty of time to spare. When you've planned a meeting at two o'clock, plan on getting there at one forty-five. Christian monks used to refer to this as *statio*, the spiritual discipline of arriving early to pray for and discern what God is doing in a meeting. *Statio*, or having gaps between events, allows you to connect your heart and mind with the will of the Spirit and to pray and think clearly about what is about to happen. It brings a sense of gravitas, or weight, to whatever it is you are about to do and clears your mind. In the off chance there's traffic or some other disruption, you have more space to arrive on time ready for a great meeting.

You cannot be compassionate when in a hurry. Even at your best, if you are in a hurry and someone needs you, it will be very difficult to do the next right thing. You will feel stressed, and you will not be fully engaged in the moment for your spouse, friend, or even a stranger who needs a hand. In this way hurrying keeps our society fragmented and disconnected and reinforces a deep lack of connection to others. Hurrying erodes our soul as it traps us in a constant state of weakness, anger, powerlessness, and resentment.

You don't need to hurry. You'll get there. Leave gaps and move with the Spirit as a sailboat moves with the wind.

Maintain Your Boundaries

When we feel we don't do enough, it's hard to respect ourselves by keeping important boundaries. When we think we are not enough, it is hard to ask for what we need. But boundaries and the ability to say no are central to living as the beloved.

Early on as a pastor, it was very hard to keep my boundaries. After all, I was the pastor of a small church: a constantly revolving door of about one hundred people. I was young, lacking any notable success in my work. I was out to prove myself, to prove that I was the pastor people needed. I said yes to everything. For a time, I was the accountant, the marketer, the web designer, the preacher, and even the worship leader. I gave everyone a ride home. I did every wedding and funeral, even when it was just a friend of a friend who attended the church. Most of that time I was paid very little and struggled to make ends meet. I was terrible at saying no because I needed every member we had. I was afraid people would leave, and I was running ragged. Add to that the casual jokes people made about the pastor "not having a real job" or "golfing all the time."

This became worse as I didn't receive a salary from the church (we were giving all the church money away to the poor—little did I know I was poor too) and felt more and more as though only I could personally meet everyone's spiritual needs. I became passive-aggressive and distant and felt guilty about disappointing all those who needed more from me when I didn't have more to give.

I didn't have clear boundaries. My desire to do well, do good, and help others was mixed up with my felt need to be accepted and admired by my church. This was a formula for disaster and almost led to complete burnout. I didn't really start succeeding in ministry until some of these church members left when I decided not to give in to their constant requests. I also began to respect my wife, my boundaries, and myself, and the church started to grow.

Brené Brown, while researching the ways that people connect deeply, found that people with clear and protected boundaries were healthier and happier. She said, "The truly committed compassion practitioners were also the most boundary-conscious people in the study. Compassionate people are boundaried people." When she discovered the results of this research, she said, "I was stunned." Musing about her own experience, Dr. Brown said before she kept her boundaries she was "sweeter—judgmental, resentful, and angry on the inside—but sweeter on the outside." But now she is more compassionate, less judgmental, and less resentful because she is "way more serious about boundaries."[1]

Respect yourself by clearly defining and keeping your boundaries, especially with your time. You are a beloved child of God and deserve respect. It's important to stick up for yourself, and to not always give in to the demands on your time. This world will want to take from you and give nothing in return. You are worth more than that. Be kind but firm, gentle but honest. We think people will be offended, but usually they are fine with it.

Live to Please God, Not People

When we live to please God, he will often draw us to hurting people. However, pleasing God doesn't mean pleasing the people he has sent us to. When you focus your life on pleasing people, you are exhausted, but when you live to please God, you will have more energy. Pleasing God and not people will allow you to be yourself, warts and all, living every day as the beloved. Because God already sees the real you and loves you just as you are, you will feel free to be vulnerable with others, growing closer to them. You cannot people please and respect yourself.

Don't pursue people. Rather, pursue personal growth while being at peace with your imperfections. Invest in yourself. Work on being the best version of you, and you will attract the right people into your life. If you go after certain people that don't care about you, you'll find your-self constantly disappointed. Build your character, and the right people will come into your life. Don't worry about building your reputation or impressing your peers. Just do what is right in the eyes of God, and you will grow in stature, honor, and favor.

Did you know in the Gospels there isn't one person Jesus didn't dis-appoint? Jesus didn't allow people to manipulate him into what they thought he should be. He had a clear mission from God and stuck to it and in doing so saved the world.

So don't live your life to please people. Live your life to please God, because he is already pleased with you. You can relax. You don't need to do more or try harder. Enjoy a time out, and remember it is morally right to be restful. Rest is where you get the big heart and fresh vision to be the best version of you.

4

YOU'RE NOT WHAT
YOU DO MORALLY

For by grace you have been saved through faith;
and that not of yourselves, it is the gift of God; not
as a result of works, so that no one may boast.
—Ephesians 2:8–9 (NASB)

What you do morally matters. I'm tempted to say what you do morally is the most important thing in the world, but it's not. It's the second most important thing in the world. Instead, your identity is the number one most important thing because in the end your identity will not only guide your actions, but your happiness as well. When you know you are the beloved of God, you will usually do good because it comes naturally, rather than do good out of willpower. When you are living in your true identity as the beloved, being a good person has nothing to do with trying harder. You do good for others because it's what is most natural to you. Therefore, the only way to be a joyful, moral person is, ironically, to let go of your identity as a moral person and embrace your identity as the beloved.

If you want to do good, but lack the power to do so, it's likely because you are trying to do good from a place of shame rather than a place of grace. You're constantly beating yourself up in the hopes you'll get your life together. Maybe you were taught to do this by your parents or through sermons you've heard in the past: "When you mess up, you beat yourself up so you won't do it again." When we do this, we are actually making things worse, not better.

Though shame can and often does push a person in the general direction of morality, his moral actions can become rigid, life thwarting, and joyless and typically lead to religiosity and hypocrisy. Because this person's identity is about being a moral person more than about being beloved, when he messes up (and he will mess up), he is now tempted to hide his mistake. In the beginning he will confess his mistakes, but because his morality is so closely linked to his identity, he won't be able to keep it up and will eventually lose that identity for one of immorality. Or he will become a person with two identities: the moral one that everyone sees and the private immoral one he sees in the mirror.

God has a better idea. Just let go and be loved right where you are. Let go of the felt need and pressure to be perfect all the time. God will form in you a moral heart only at the point where you are at peace with your flaws and imperfections, because it's only there you receive grace. When you are at peace with your shortcomings and don't link them to your identity, then it is not so painful to work on those things with others. You'll stop saying to yourself, "I will be worthy of love when I earn it." Right there in that place, unearned love from God and others will foster gratitude and joy in your heart that will lead to altruism and goodness.

When you truly believe you are loved by God just as you are, you can let go of your works and good deeds as an identity and inherit the power to actually become a good person. Yes, it takes time for our heart and actions to change, but in the end, people who feel loved by God and others are moral and happy. You are not your morality. You are beloved.

You Can't Lose His Love

I once read a story about a young girl in the foster-care program. She desperately wanted to have a real mom and dad, a home where she belonged, a place where she was wanted just as she was. She wanted a house and maybe a dog. She wanted to get tucked in at night. When other kids asked where her mom and dad were, she wanted the lie she always told—"They're at home waiting for me"—to be true. Because she was getting a little older, her fear grew that this would never happen for her. She'd always be an unwanted wanderer. After all, everyone knows big kids never get adopted.

She was taken out for "test drives" by various foster parents, all good people who were doing more than many others had done, but in the end she was always seen as having too much baggage. To be honest, she was not a particularly good kid, and when she went too far over the line, the family would send her back to the agency and say something like, "She's just too much."

Her entire young life was like this, never settled. She would only belong if she acted right. She had to earn her family's love, and when she misbehaved she'd lose that family. She'd go back into the foster program, where she would wait and hope to get another chance to prove herself.

Then out of nowhere a couple, very different from the others, decided they would adopt her forever. They said, plain as day, she would always be their daughter—no matter what. When they got her, they told her there was nothing she could do to be sent back to the agency. She was home now. She was theirs for the long haul, and they were going to love her for better or worse. They even went as far as writing up a contract they all signed, agreeing she would be with them forever. They framed that contract and put it on her wall where she could see it every day.

She tested the promise. Yes, she did some really bad things to prove their faithfulness. But they cared for her, loved her, disciplined her, held and defined boundaries, and yet never gave up on her. When she realized her parents' love wasn't earned, she became a terrific kid. She found a true home where she wasn't some well-behaved guest. This was her home and her family now. Her life was never the same because she had people who said, "You belong before you behave."

Do you ever feel like this girl in your relationship with God? It's easy to think we are his beloved children because of our good deeds, our moral compass, or our spiritual trophies. But when we mess up, as we always do, we feel deep shame, confusion, and may even leave or lose our faith. Many of us are on a "holy-coaster," never finding our home in our true spiritual family. We have spiritual highs where we feel close to God and others, then lows where we don't even know if we believe in God or think he's abandoned us because of our mistakes, or feel isolated from others. We feel we are not family in the house of God, only well-behaved guests.

This will never do. You belong in spite of your flaws and imperfections.

All of our sin and spiritual pain begins with a haunting inner voice that says, *You're not enough. You don't belong. Try harder. You don't do enough. You're a screw-up. God is ashamed of you. Hide your imperfections.* Many of these thoughts are often unconscious feelings, but if we talk about them or pay attention to them, we see they are strong. They are at the heart of many of the very actions we are ashamed of. They are at the heart of our self-rejection. And self-rejection leads to death because we agree with the voice of the Accuser rather than the voice of the Father. Henri Nouwen put it best in a sermon he gave at the Crystal Cathedral. He said:

> Over the years, I have come to realize that the greatest trap in our life is not success, popularity, or power, but self-rejection. Success, popularity, and power can indeed present a great temptation, but their seductive quality often comes from the way they are part of the much larger temptation to self-rejection. When we have come to

believe in the voices that call us worthless and unlovable, then success, popularity, and power are easily perceived as attractive solutions. The real trap, however, is self-rejection. As soon as someone accuses me or criticizes me, as soon as I am rejected, left alone, or abandoned, I find myself thinking, "Well, that proves once again that I am a nobody" . . . [My dark side says] I am no good . . . I deserve to be pushed aside, forgotten, rejected, and abandoned. Self-rejection is the greatest enemy of the spiritual life because it contradicts the sacred voice that calls us the "Beloved." Being the Beloved constitutes the core truth of our existence.

Let go of those soul-harming words, because they are not from God. God says over you, "My dear child, there is therefore no condemnation for those who are in Christ Jesus. I'm not here to condemn you. I'm here to give you life and peace" (see Rom. 8:1). All joy and life comes from the voice that says, "You are my beloved child and I'm proud of you. You and I will get through life together. When you mess up, I've got your back. I wish you could see the future I have planned for you. It's amazing!" This is why it is written that the Devil is called "the accuser of our brethren" (Rev. 12:10 KJV) and the Holy Spirit is called "the Comforter" (John 14:26 KJV). God is always on your side.

Love what is good and hate what is evil, but never let your identity as a moral person become the reason for personal worth and belonging. If we find our identity in what we do and don't do morally, messing up causes us to believe we are no longer worthy of love, compassion, belonging, and deep connection. We become afraid of reaching out to others in our woundedness. We feel isolated, alone, and ashamed. These emotions won't make you a better person.

We cannot allow our identity to be rooted in a do-gooders report card either. You may have drawn up one of these report cards before. You measure all the stuff you're proud of against all the ways you've messed up or things you don't like about yourself and hope you've got a B+. This is an easy temptation to fall into. We all do it. This report card is based on pride and is rooted in our own efforts. It ultimately leads to exhaustion.

Throwing the report card away is the best thing we can do because good deeds come from a heart fully alive in God's love. We cannot say, "I only belong when I'm good enough." Instead our self-talk should be, "I belong in spite of my imperfections. I'm loved by God."

Give up your identity in what you do and live in the freedom of God's love and forgiveness. You are not what you do or what you've done. You are what Christ did for you. He loves you.

> You are not what you do or what you've done. You are what Christ did for you.

After years of ministry, I'm realizing more and more that moral people are good because they are emotionally healthy; they live vulnerable, imperfect, yet beautiful, lives rooted in a deep sense of safety. Being secure in their identity gives them the freedom to ask for help when they need it. They do not allow their egos to get inflated when their lives bear fruit. They are unlikely to even talk about themselves as moral or immoral. They are loved. They've let go of worrying about being perfect and humbly desire to do the next right thing. They in no way allow people to dictate to them who they are, because they know who they are.

You don't need more guilt or shame. You need encouragement. You don't need to wallow because of something in your past or because you keep messing up. You need to hear the voice that is calling out to you, "Beloved child, don't give up. I'm with you and I'll never stop cheering you on. Keep reaching out for me and for others. You are wanted. You belong."

In the shakiness of living, remember one simple thing: you are not what you've done, and you are not what you do. You are a beloved child of God. No one can take that from you. You didn't earn it. You've never lived a day where that wasn't true. God absolutely adores you. He was there when you breathed your first breath. He'll be there to catch that breath when you die. You are beloved.

Not by Works

When I started college, I thought being a Christian meant that if I didn't mess up too much, I could be a child of God. At eighteen I had a list of things I was sure would land me in the "backslidden" category, which would put me in danger of hell. This list pretty much consisted of premarital sex, cussing too much, and smoking or doing drugs (along with the more obvious but unlikely sins such as murder, rape, etc.). I didn't realize it at the time, but I essentially believed I only belonged to God because I didn't do these things. There was a nervousness in my heart that I was dangling by a thread and that my faith ultimately boiled down to a system of sin management.

Because I attended a Christian school, many of these assumptions were challenged in my theology classes. It was during this time one of my dear friends (whom we would say was "on fire" for God) called me. He had a ministry at his house for teenagers and was working hard to help these kids get their lives back on track. He was and is a good man. He said, "Bobby, I'm so disappointed. I had these kids over at my house. We had an amazing time praying together and studying the Bible. All of them prayed to receive Christ. It was such a great moving of the Spirit. But then a few days later when I went to visit them at the high school, they were out in the alley smoking weed. One day they were destined for heaven, and now they're destined for hell!"

Trying to relax him, I jokingly said to my friend, "Too bad they didn't just die between the two events, because then they'd be in heaven forever." To my shock and dismay, my friend didn't know I was joking and agreed with me!

Because we shared almost identical theologies at the time, this one conversation became a mirror for how we both viewed the character of God. I began to ask myself, "Is God only with me so long as I don't get too far out of line? Is that the kind of grace the Bible talked about?"

Over the years, as I've learned the true meaning of grace, I've found that my behavior became better the less worried I was about "losing my salvation." The more I cared about being in God's presence and worshiping him, the less I thought about sin. Feeling safe in the idea that God wasn't going to take away his promise of heaven actually made me more kind and less worried and transformed my mind to stop thinking about sin so much. I found the less I thought about managing sin, the less tempted I was to sin. I found the more I meditated on God's love and blessing, the more driven I was to honor God and treat my neighbor with dignity and love.

Paul wrote about how he used to think he was made right with God by living a perfect life. He said he might have bragged about how closely he followed the law, doing everything right. After all, he was a moral pillar. But then he said, "All of that is garbage compared to the righteousness I have by faith!" (see Phil. 3:7–9). Faith in what? Faith in God's love for all humanity as exemplified in the cross and resurrection. He explained in another letter how we belong to God not because of our good deeds, but because of grace. I love the way *The Message* translates these verses:

> Now God has us where he wants us, with all the time in this world and the next to shower grace and kindness upon us in Christ Jesus. Saving is all his idea, and all his work. All we do is trust him enough to let him do it. It's God's gift from start to finish! We don't play the major role. If we did, we'd probably go around bragging that we'd done the whole thing! (Eph. 2:7–8)

Without grace, our good works become a type of soul-killing legalism, a lifeless system of trying harder to earn the affection or approval of God and man. This system is made of saints and sinners—those who are in because of their good deeds and those who are out because they don't follow the rules. But grace says, "No matter who you are, trust your life to God in Christ Jesus, and he'll get you where you need to be. Have patience in the in-between. You are God's beloved child and he has you by the hand."

The first step to living full of God's energy is simply believing you are loved even when you mess up. Give yourself grace. Be kind to yourself. You are not what you do. You are not what you've done. You are not what has been done to you. You are the beloved, and that's very good news. Heaven is your home.

Few people articulated this idea better than Brennan Manning. He was a priest who dedicated most of his years to a contemplative life serving the poor and prisoners—an experience that ultimately culminated in his writing his famous *The Ragamuffin Gospel*. Just before his death, he gave a sermon I've never forgotten. He said something like:

> In the forty-eight years since I was first ambushed by Jesus . . . and then literally the thousands of hours of prayer, meditation, silence, and solitude over those years, I am now utterly convinced that . . . the Lord Jesus is going to ask us one question, and only one question: "Did you believe that I loved you? That I waited for you day after day? That I longed to hear the sound of your voice?" The real believers there will answer, "Yes, Jesus! I believed in your love, and I tried to shape my life as a response to it."[1]

I think when we get to heaven we are going to be very surprised by who is there with us. We are going to look around and see the same people Jesus invited to his table: the hoodlums, the thieves and tax collectors, the prostitutes, sitting and celebrating grace with him in eternity. Manning painted the picture like this:

> Because salvation is by grace through faith, I believe that among the countless number of people standing in front of the throne and in front of the Lamb, dressed in white robes and holding palms in their hands, I shall see the prostitute from the Kit-Kat Ranch in Carson City, Nevada, who tearfully told me she could find no other employment to support her two-year-old son. I shall see the woman who had an abortion and is haunted by guilt and remorse but did the best she could faced with grueling alternatives; the businessman besieged with

debt who sold his integrity in a series of desperate transactions; the insecure clergyman addicted to being liked, who never challenged his people from the pulpit and longed for unconditional love; the sexually abused teen molested by his father and now selling his body on the street, who, as he falls asleep each night after his last "trick" whispers the name of the unknown God he learned about in Sunday school; the death-bed convert who for decades had his cake and ate it, broke every law of God and man, wallowed in lust and raped the earth.

"But how?" we ask.

Then the voice says, "They have washed their robes and made them white in the blood of the Lamb."

There they are. There *we* are—the multitude who so wanted to be faithful, who at times got defeated, soiled by life, and bested by trials, wearing the bloodied garments of life's tribulations, but through it all clung to the faith.[2]

That's good news for us, because on those days I feel I have let people down, or let God down, I'm reminded that God will get me where I need to be. It just takes time. I'm reminded that if I continue to love what is good and have my identity firmly planted in God's love, I will grow naturally into godliness. But in the in-between, working hard to be the best version of me, I can relax when I fall short. I can know that I won't always be this way, and that every day God is getting me one step closer to my destiny. I don't have to worry about my shortcomings. I am loved and I belong.

Intimacy with God

Knowing God means having a deep, abiding, personal friendship with him. He is a genuine friend and father. Personal growth means to further realize and experience this deep spiritual friendship. Though comparing our relationship with God to a relationship between lovers may seem inappropriate, it really does fit the profound feeling that many have in their experiences with God.

Like two young lovers, you wouldn't have to tell a young man, "Kiss her," "Buy her flowers," or "Tell your friends about how great she is." You wouldn't need to remind the girl, "Call him," "Hug him," "Say yes the next time he wants to go on a date." No, they can't even hang up the phone. Likewise, when your life and experience with God is true and deep, doing what is good and right comes naturally. A true spiritual relationship with God fosters within us the desire to be with him, love him, and endure hell on earth for him if he would ask.

Have you lost your first love? Do you feel shame more than grace, legalism more than freedom? Do you feel like you are just surviving, always trying harder, but it's not enough? We all feel this way sometimes in our spiritual walk. Feeling like we're never good enough, always having to prove ourselves to God, or feeling like we're always catching up—these notions drain the soul because they are the opposite of the joy that comes from intimacy. They kill our inner life with God.

Holiness is based on intimacy, not willpower. The satisfied soul overflows like a fountain with living water, blessing all who see it and drink from it. When we feel and know God's love in spite of failings, we are encouraged and joyful. We can't help but give God our best.

In the romantic Christmas film *Love Actually*, there is a side narrative about a middle-aged married couple. I think it's one of the saddest depictions in any movie I've seen. It's too real. The husband and wife seem happily married, as any couple would after being married for so many years, but the viewer finds out quickly the husband is secretly having an affair. For Christmas, he decides to buy his secret lover a beautiful necklace, an expensive gold chain with a jeweled gold heart at its end.

One day, as she's putting socks away in his dresser, his wife finds this now-hidden gift. Thinking it's for her, she smiles widely and puts it back in the dresser. She had joked with him earlier, "After thirteen years of 'Mr. Oh, but you love scarfs,' my expectations are not that high for a great gift." Now, for days, she smiles at her husband, so looking forward to the beautiful gift. She truly is his treasure, she believes.

When Christmas comes, she opens the box he gives her quickly, smiling, only to find a Joni Mitchell CD.

A long, silent pause . . .

She instantly understands the necklace was for another woman and not for her. The husband gave his treasure to the one he loved and gave "what passes" to his wife.

Our relationship with God can look like this. After years of knowing him, it's easy to fall out of love and passion. We are still moral people in general, but we lack deep intimacy. When intimacy is lacking with God, "what passes" is what our morality is for him. It's not something we do in response to his love. It's not a natural outflow of what he is doing in our inner lives. It's simply a morality that suffices. It's a Joni Mitchell CD.

Confess Good Stuff

The Bible tells us to confess our sins, but did you know Paul, the author of most of the New Testament, never told anyone to confess his or her sins? Yes, he taught that sin is death, that we are all sinners, and that only Christ can save us from our sin. But he never gave the confession of sin as a spiritual discipline or practice in the Christian life. In fact, there are only two places where confessing sin is mentioned in the New Testament: once in the book of James and the other in 1 John. Both of these books, incidentally, were written well after Paul wrote his letters. Again, I want to reiterate the Bible still teaches us to confess our sins, but Paul himself didn't. Did he do us a disservice?

Paul wrote about grace, resurrection, justification, and imputed righteousness by Christ. In 2 Corinthians he said, "God made him who had no sin to be sin for us, so that in him we might become the righteousness of God" (5:21). What if, after we asked people to confess their sin, we then asked them to confess they are "the righteousness of God

60

in Christ Jesus"? What if, when we did something we weren't proud of, we responded with, "I am the righteousness of God in Christ Jesus," rather than, "I'm a rotten, terrible sinner." To me one sounds like healthy remorse ("I'm a new creation. This isn't me."), and the other sounds like the kind of shame that is the root of so much addiction, dysfunction, and pathology. One sounds like something said by faith and grace, and the other sounds like religiosity and legalism.

The Bible says the Devil is "the persecutor of the brethren," and Christ is our attorney. The Bible says the Enemy comes to condemn, but Christ comes that we may have life and have it in abundance (John 10:10). The word that is most used for the Holy Spirit is *Comforter*.

What if by always talking about how rotten, horrible, and sinful we are, we are pleasing not God but the Devil? What if, when we say we are sinners without confessing, "I am the righteousness of God in Christ Jesus," we are agreeing with the Enemy and not God? What if we began to confess the promises of the Bible over ourselves rather than the accusations of the Devil? What if we said,

- "I'm not what I do. I am the righteousness of God in Christ Jesus."
- "I'm not what I do. I am chosen, called to his good purpose."
- "I'm not what I do. I am favored."
- "I'm above and not beneath. I'm the head and not the tail."
- "I'm anointed."
- "I'm set apart."
- "I'm destined for salvation."

I originally heard the idea of confessing "I am the righteousness of God in Christ Jesus" from a Singaporean pastor named Joseph Prince. He was sitting with a group of pastors sharing with us what he'd learned in ministry, and this was one of my big takeaways. He was talking about how pornography addiction had become such a huge issue in their church. Many young men and women were struggling with the deep sense of shame that comes with it. He instructed his pastors to teach these people to shift their language from constantly confessing how sinful they were to declaring, "I am the righteousness of God in Christ Jesus." He said more than any other spiritual practice, this one had helped people break the bonds of pornography addiction because they were reinforcing an identity rooted in grace rather than one rooted in shame.

It's healthy to pay attention to our self-talk. The way we view ourselves and the way we talk to ourselves in our heads has a huge impact on our level of energy and on our behavior. Shame has no place in the life of a follower of Jesus. We must understand that no one is perfect, and that God alone has the power to break the bondage of sin in our life. By affirming your scriptural identity as the beloved through practices like praying the Creed of the Beloved, you will come to the firm knowledge that by being chosen by God, you are marked for salvation. You are not what you do. You are not your good deeds, bad deeds, or your moral trophies. You are the righteousness of God, a beloved child of the Lord.

So today, you can relax. You are doing so much better than you think. Everyone has moral issues they're wrestling with, but few people share these issues with others. Every day you are getting closer to your destiny. God's not going to abandon you when you mess up. Be kind to your soul. Speak grace and peace over yourself, not condemnation. Let go of your identity in what you do and instead take hold of the fact that in spite of messing up sometimes, you're terrific and God adores you.

5

YOU'RE NOT WHAT YOU DO—BUT YOU'LL DO GREAT THINGS

*I'd rather attempt to do something great and fail
than to attempt to do nothing and succeed.*
—Robert H. Schuller

You are going to do great things in your life. I am so passionate about Christians finding an identity rooted in God's love, because I know that's ultimately the only way they will fulfill their destiny. Confusion about identity is the main reason why Christians give up on the great callings God places on them. They compare themselves to the accomplishments of others. They think, *I haven't earned an education* or *I don't have any business experience.* As a pastor I had to learn very quickly that if I wanted to succeed in ministry I couldn't compare myself to other pastors or their churches or their budgets. I had to just be me, and that would be the most successful version of me.

When our identity is rooted in being the beloved, we can do whatever we want without feeling pressure from society. We are free to pursue a big vision despite our critics. We become people in love with possibility and don't worry as much about failure, because failure has nothing to do with belonging. When we are focused on being God's beloved, we simply desire to do what God wants. If he calls us to do nothing for a season, that's okay.

This freedom evaporates when we think we are not worthy of love and belonging and need to prove ourselves. If we remain constantly rooted in the idea that we are what we do, we will simply do too much and will burn out. In other words, we get emotional energy when we stop worrying about being amazing, perfect, impressive, or relevant and just decide to do the awesome thing God wants from us. When this happens, we are able to focus our energy on that one thing rather than a bunch of things at the same time. We go from victory to victory and get encouraged along the way. We don't allow setbacks to destroy us and instead gain a new resilience.

If the first component to having a vibrant energetic life is identity, the second is passion—that is, having a big dream or desire and really going for it with all your heart. I'm interjecting it here because my concern about letting go of what you do as part of your identity can feel like I'm saying, "Just give up." I'm not. The only thing I want you to give up is being overwhelmed, cluttered, exhausted with proving yourself to others, and people pleasing. Boundaries, self-respect, and loads of spiritual energy are required for you to do the great things God has called you to. In fact, in a Christian worldview, desire is at the heart of your faith.

Many Christians lack passion. They experience setbacks that cause them to give up on their dreams. After too many failures they think *they* are a failure and find themselves struggling with depression. Or, at best, the nagging feeling that they settled. This, too, is rooted in shame and the idea that "I am what I do." If you are in that place, it might be that your self-talk is, "I am a failure." Perhaps it's time you let go of that and with abandon just start dreaming again. Having a big dream or desire, living every day with passion and zeal, is central to the Christian walk.

As children, we dreamed all the time. We had big ideas and goals, and we didn't allow anyone to sway us. One week we wanted to be an astronaut, the next we wanted to be a ninja. We didn't care what the pay was. As children, we were full of energy, life, and passion because we hadn't lost a sense of wonder. As children, we saw the world as a boundless canvas of opportunity and did not limit our thinking.

We start life so full of energy, but after enough loneliness, rejection, and suffering, we take a more realistic view of the world. This is where our spirituality finds itself in mortal danger, because in a Christian worldview our desire is our spirituality. After all, Jesus said, "Unless you . . . become like little children, you will never enter the kingdom of heaven" (Matt. 18:3).

Perhaps you thought Christianity was all about being morose and boring and following a bunch of rules and rites. Perhaps you thought being a spiritual person meant getting rid of passion altogether. Not so. Your soul is made to desire.

Every human being is made in the image of God and brings a bit of his power into this world. Being born is a crazy affair. We enter the world with no rules or boundaries, naked and covered in blood, screaming. No baby comes into the hospital room saying, "Father, Mother, so nice to meet you. When you get a second, I desire something." In fact, a newborn baby expresses raw spirit, fire, and passion. Whether aflame or barely flickering, that same passion remains in our hearts, and it is this passion that has fueled some of the greatest good and evil in the world.

Perhaps to be born again means to regain some of this fire we had as children. Perhaps we are meant to clean off the many barnacles of societal taboos and pressures placed on us by the world. Christianity teaches us to focus our passion on what is good. It certainly doesn't teach us to get rid of it. The greatest women and men who have made a difference in history have been passionate people. Simply look to leaders such as Dorothy Day, Dr. King, or Billy Graham to see very clearly those who dream and live with passion. The big difference is their passion doesn't result in destructive behavior. Rather, it's totally devoted to God's call.

I'm startled by how many American Christians will criticize another believer as being too emotional, as if being emotional were ungodly or somehow a bad thing. Yes, emotions can cloud our reason and cause us to be unwise at times. That's certainly not prudent. But you also can't be like Jesus without being at least a little emotional. When Jesus preached against religious hypocrisy, he was emotional. When he saw his friend Lazarus dead in a tomb, he was emotional. When he turned over the moneychangers' tables, when he prayed in the garden of Gethsemane, when he gave his life on the cross for his friends, he was emotional. Isn't the crucifixion called *The Passion*?

Being emotional and passionate is a good thing; it's the very definition of being spiritual. But it's only good to the point that those emotions and passions are mastered. Mastered doesn't mean "turned down." It means your emotions are focused and trained, like a laser. You are passionate about helping others. You are passionate in your prayer. You are passionate in your love for your children or your friends. Your emotion is an inner fire directed toward fighting what you are afraid of, toward generosity, and toward spiritual growth.

The axiom is true that "Emotions make great slaves but terrible masters." The Catholic priest and theologian Ronald Rolheiser used the analogy of Mother Teresa and Janis Joplin to explain that point. Janis Joplin was passionate, on fire for life and music. She made some amazing art. She put on incredible shows. Everywhere she went she brought energy and power. She was a broken soul, though. Her brokenness drew people and she had thousands of fans, but this only exacerbated her problem. She needed real love and friendship but in the end hurt many of those around her and destroyed herself because of her out-of-control passion. She burned for burning's sake and, like an explosion, died at the young age of twenty-seven. There's something admirable about Janis Joplin; like many passionate people, she was attractive if destructive. Not someone to emulate, but still endearing. Yet like many bright flames, she burned out quickly.

It's hard not to wonder what might have happened if Janis had met Jesus and trusted her life to him.

Janis Joplin and Mother Teresa had the same fire and passion for life. They were bold, courageous, and very emotional. The difference is Janis Joplin allowed her emotions to control her and destroy her life. Mother Teresa, however, controlled and focused those emotions to give life to others. Few alive had more passion than she, but those emotions were a blessing and not a curse.

Mother Teresa was an Albanian nun, petite in stature, who answered a call from God to go to India and serve. She began teaching at a Catholic school for young, affluent religious kids while watching other children—unwanted children—dying alone in the streets. As she watched this happen day after day, it ate away at her. Pulled by the spirit of God, she left her prestigious role at the school to simply be present with those who were dying. Like Janis Joplin, Mother Teresa was a fireball, but fearless, focused, and a follower of Jesus.

Once, during an interview, she sat holding a young child who was in pain, dying. This little girl urinated on herself and on Teresa. In disgust, the reporter turned to the cameraman and, thinking Mother Teresa wouldn't hear, whispered, "Ugh, I wouldn't do that for a million dollars."

Mother Teresa did hear it. She yelled at the reporter, "Neither would I!"

You can see it, can't you—the dramatic scene of a Westerner disgusted by human suffering and uninterested in helping? In contrast, because of her desire to never let anyone die alone, Teresa changed the world. She embodied the words of author Finley Peter Dunne: "comfort th' afflicted, and afflicts th' comfortable."[1]

On another occasion Mother Teresa was invited to a large gathering at the White House as the guest of honor, sitting next to then-president and First Lady Bill and Hillary Clinton. She was asked to give a speech on world peace, and she agreed. When she came up to the podium, her first line was, "Abortion has become the greatest destroyer of peace, because it destroys two lives—the life of the child and the conscience of the mother." She continued, "Let us thank our parents for wanting us, for loving us, for giving us the joy of living . . . You are priceless to God himself."[2] Despite your views on abortion, you must admit this was a very brave thing to say in the Clinton White House. That passion carried Mother Teresa into a victorious life.

We've all had moments where we really let loose. Maybe with a group of friends or at a wedding, we do something absolutely unlike our normal behavior. We jump into a pool fully clothed or make our first attempt to give a breakdancing circle a try. These moments—when we just stop caring and do something really fun, where we let go of our reputations and live boldly, even for a moment—are often when we feel the most life and joy.

We're always struggling with both the desire to fit in and the desire to be unique. We want to be an example, and yet we don't want to be uncomfortable. We want to do something crazy, but we don't want to be socially awkward. We all feel this way, but following Jesus means you need at least a small touch of crazy.

You are not what you do, so why are you worried about failing? You are not what you do, so do something great! We have to fail at least ten times for every success we experience. Maybe you think, *If I fail, then I'm a failure.* Absolutely not! Failure only belongs to the courageous, to those who try. Those who never fail are those who never attempt to do anything great with their lives. They live safe "lives of quiet desperation," as Thoreau stated in *Walden.*

Not you—you would rather attempt to do something great and fail than attempt to do nothing and succeed. Be zealous, on fire for God and for what he wants. Be a fearless warrior for good. Build, dream, make, and proclaim. Do not think God wants you to simply fill an empty pew and live within a sleepy rote religiosity. Rather, he wants you to burn for him. To paraphrase evangelist and author Leonard Ravenhill, God cares more about filling empty hearts than he does about filling empty pews. It's the truth. You need to be passionate. You need spiritual energy—desire—if you are going to do great things for God.

In other words, your passion is what defines your spirituality. What you do with your inner fire is your spirituality. To be spiritual means to passionately desire something. You might have good desires or bad desires, but if you desire something, you are spiritual. Spiritual does not mean you are godly, however. It means you are energetic and full of life. Janis Joplin was very spiritual, and so was Mother Teresa. One had a destructive spirituality and the other had a healthy, godly spirituality.

Ironically, the Christian who rarely sins, yet also has done very little for God and has little passion or desire, is not spiritual. He's spiritually dead. Dead people don't sin, you know. So we don't want to be sinful, but we don't want to be stoic, indifferent, or bored either. We want to be like Jesus—full of power, life, and courage.

> Your passion is what defines your spirituality.

An identity rooted in being the beloved frees you to be spiritual and passionate. If you start dreaming and start burning with zeal, there may be a small voice in your head that says, *What are people going to think?* An identity rooted in what people think about you will be the death of your spirituality, because you cannot be both passionate and worried. You can't live a life for God but not want to offend anyone. Proclaiming the Creed of the Beloved can help you find absolute freedom to burn with passion for the Lord.

Start Dreaming Again

You used to do it all the time. It doesn't matter if the dream is silly or even imaginary. Writing things on a paper napkin or daydreaming about your future is good for you, because even though you may never do those things, you are thinking about what is possible. You are broadening your vision to include more than what you're currently experiencing. Do that enough and you just might land on something that can really change your life and the lives of others. Build a dream, even a small one, and that dream will build you.

It's been said, "A thousand-mile journey begins with a single step." When you've been in that place of low energy for a while, it's easy to feel stuck. Yes, God always has big plans for you, but don't let that stop you from getting started on something new and fresh in your life. Little victories count and are so important to keep you moving in the direction of positive change in your life. Every milestone you reach shows you that you have more power than you thought and encourages you to go farther and do more. So dream big, but don't be afraid to start small.

There's nothing wrong with taking small steps. In fact, small steps are one of the best ways to stop procrastinating. Very often we feel overwhelmed by whatever project is before us, so we just eat, surf the Web, or do some discouraged napping. If you're trying to work out more, just go to the gym for ten minutes. If you're trying to read your Bible more, just read one verse. That way it doesn't seem so daunting, and if you do a little more . . . it's extra credit.

In a recent TED talk, Amy Morin, an acclaimed psychologist, shared how one of her clients struggled with depression and was severely overweight. It was hard for him to do anything. His weight was at a place where he now had diabetes, further complicating his state of mind. One day his vision started blurring and he went almost blind because of his blood sugar. This tragedy culminated in him making a real change.

He began with one small step: instead of drinking a two-liter bottle of Pepsi every night, he started drinking a two-liter bottle of *Diet* Pepsi. This had an instant effect on his blood-sugar level. Galvanized by this little victory, he decided to have a healthier snack like beef jerky instead of ice cream before he went to bed. This made a big difference too. One day, he saw an old exercise bike for sale and bought it for twenty dollars. He put it in front of his TV so he could ride it while watching. He started losing weight quickly. One day, while riding that bike, his blurry vision became a little clearer. This big milestone became the first of many victories in his life. Now he's fit and healthy and excited about the next win.[3]

Anyone can feel overwhelmed by a big dream. But believe God can get you to your dream, and start small. Those little victories will create passion and joy.

God Has a Great Future For You!

Sometimes we lose our fire or passion because we feel shame about our past. Perhaps you've been divorced more than once or you dropped out of school. You feel you were a bad parent or you just never made it in your career the way you hoped you would. It's easy to think that because you haven't lived the life you wanted, you somehow don't deserve a good future from God. This feeling is shame. Don't let regrets about your past keep you from being a passionate follower of Jesus and from having big desires in your heart. Be vulnerable and honest about your past, but then leave it in the past and focus on the present.

Some of the greatest leaders in the world lead from a place of vulnerability. Their past does not define them or control them. Their past becomes an important part of their story and helps them help others in a better way. The more secret and embarrassed you are about your past, the more it controls and defines you. The more you share your past with others, the more authority you have to lead from experience. People will also relate to you better. We all prefer "leaders with a limp," as author John Wimber called them.

Remember, whatever you've done in your past, it has been paid for. You are not a slave anymore. When Jesus said, "It is finished," he meant it. God has given you a new name and has adopted you into his family. He is not ashamed to be seen with you and longs to be with you. He's proud of you, and so am I!

You are not a failure. Failure and loss are hard to endure and can rob us of our passion. When we have a big setback in life, it's easy to get down and stuck in a rut. Our thoughts can enter a relentless cycle of what-ifs and dwell on regrets. It's hard to break out of this kind of thinking because it keeps us in an emotional trap. Willie Jolley, the bestselling author and motivational speaker, said something that helps me when I get caught in this trap: "Every setback is a setup for a comeback." It reminds me of one of my dad's greatest lines: "If you're down to nothing, God is up to something."

It's true. The way to break free from what-if thinking is to change our focus from self-pity to possibility. It doesn't have to be probable or reasonable, just possible. As we focus on possibility, a dream begins to build in our hearts and allows God's energy to flow.

A few years ago my wife was having some major health problems with neuropathy and stomach issues. It started out as just a little thing but over the years became worse and worse. Soon it was so bad she could hardly eat anything, and the doctors seemed completely unable to help. Hannah's dad, a successful businessman, offered to pay for her to get an assessment and treatment at the Mayo Clinic, one of the finest clinics in the world. After months of testing and review they told her, "Hannah, we're sorry. We can't help you, and you're only going to get worse. You're just going to have to get used to this."

This news was such a horrible blow to both of us. She was already so miserable, and I was miserable for her. In many ways we were being told, "Life, as you know it, is over. Just get used to it."

But a few years later, we discovered a new medicine—one the doctors never told us was available—and today, Hannah is completely well. That first day doctors told us it was hopeless, but God had something else in mind. We had held on to the dream that Hannah could be well, and we never stopped searching.

Doctors are wonderful, but they will be the first to tell you they don't know everything. There is always hope. There are always new medical discoveries being made every day. And more important, we serve the Great Healer who loves to do miracles.

No matter what setback you face, don't get caught in negative thinking. Trust in God, and put your hope in him. There is a way forward. Be alive. Live with enthusiasm for everything. The word *enthusiasm* means "God within." When you live with passion, you feel alive and are more in tune with heaven. Heaven's a passionate place, after all. You'll be glad that you lived with big dreams and lots of energy, making a few mistakes along the way, rather than just being safe all the time. To paraphrase author and speaker Tony Campolo, "I don't know about you, but I don't want to tiptoe through life only to arrive safely at death." Being passionate is being spiritual. Desiring things. Wanting more from life, and refining your fire with the Word of God. Do your best to walk as Jesus did. You will feel more alive and have more energy.

You are not what you do, and you are not what you have or haven't accomplished. You are not a failure. If you let go of your identity in what you do, you will no longer be shackled by the pain and embarrassment of failure. Failure to you will simply become one more lesson getting you closer to your destiny. You are loved, called, blessed, and favored.

6

YOU'RE NOT WHAT
YOU HAVE

Spiritual identity means we are not what we do or what
people say about us. And we are not what we have.
We are the beloved daughters and sons of God.
—Henri Nouwen

What Do You Daydream About?

Have you ever felt that, because of your lack of designer clothing, a beautiful car, or financial status, you didn't matter as much as those who had them? Perhaps since our culture values youth and beauty above all else, you felt below average or even ugly, as though you didn't have the same personal value as those who were young and beautiful. These feelings are the result of people finding their value in what they have instead of who they are. By turning material wealth, beauty, and fashion into the foundations for personal value, culture naturally degenerates into hollow recreational sex, addiction, and always nihilism. People cease to be human because they believe they are what they have.

> You are not what you have.
> You are not what you have lost.
> You are beloved.

Treasure is the thing that matters most to us. It's the thing we think about. It's what we daydream about when waiting in line at the DMV. What we treasure is a reflection of our soul. It tells a lot about our story, our memories, and often works as a way we hold onto something or someone that may have passed long ago. When you treasure something, you often keep it in a safe place, or you may show it to your friends when they visit you at home. I have a crystal *Jonah and the Whale* sculpture given to me by my grandpa when I played the part of Jonah in a third-grade school musical. He came to see me in that play and afterward sent me the sculpture because, in his words, "I was so impressed by your performance." I doubt I would have won an Oscar for my performance. Yet as an adult this little crystal whale has tremendous value for me—as it should. It's connected to a great memory and a person I loved.

What do you treasure? I know what God treasures. Without a doubt he treasures you. When you desire God more than money, health, success, or acclaim, your relationship with him is sustaining and vibrant, and everything else in life gets healthier. And sometimes God gives those things in greater abundance. When you know and trust him, you know good things are always coming your way, even if the current circumstances are not the best.

Jesus said, "Seek first His kingdom and His righteousness, and all these things will be added to you" (Matt. 6:33 NASB). "All these things" in this context is referring to material blessings. I don't think it means you'll be rich; Jesus is talking specifically here about what we eat, drink, and wear. The irony is if that's the reason we treasure him, he's not first. He's second. So if we seek after God's kingdom and righteousness, the promise of Scripture is we won't have to worry about "all these [material] things," because "your heavenly Father knows that you need all these things" (v. 32 NASB). He will provide. Put God first, and he'll put you first.

When things like money and acclaim are our top priorities, life will lose its flavor, and in that bland state of being, we will have no joy. Without God, friends, and family, your life will lose meaning, and you'll be confused. It doesn't matter how much wealth you have.

"Where Your Treasure Is, There Your Heart Will Be"

Too often, workaholics willingly abandon their family or friends in the pursuit of financial security. They say, "When I have enough to get out of the rat race, then I'll dial back and spend time with the people who need me." God will never bless these people until they make a change in their thinking. Even if they get to the place where they have enough, too many moments and memories will be lost, and no amount of financial freedom will appease the feelings of loss and regret. Parents die. Kids grow up. Friends move. Don't miss out on being with them, and don't allow money to be your greatest treasure and desire.

One way to see how we daydream about money is to simply look at the game of Monopoly. Monopoly was an evolution of something called *The Landlord's Game*, originally designed for political reasons to show how "unfair and dangerous" the system of renting was becoming in Atlantic City. The idea backfired as people enjoyed the fantasy of real estate ownership, entrepreneurism, and capitalism. The game evolved over time and in the 1930s during the Depression, Parker Brothers released the final version, Monopoly, with huge success. Though people were desperately looking for work and barely had enough to eat, Monopoly gave ambitious Americans some solace and fantasy in an opportunity-lacking economy.

Playing Monopoly is fun because it allows us to live out our day-dreams of being rich and successful. There's nothing wrong with a game of Monopoly, of course, but it reveals our unconscious fantasizing about money. People think about what it would be like to not have to work, to be able to dress in whatever designer clothing they want, to travel and be free of responsibilities. It's also ultimately saying, "What I have now is not enough. If I get more, I'll have the good life." It doesn't matter that many of the most famous and wealthy people seem to struggle with depression, addiction, and a warped moral compass. Most people would very much like to learn the hard way that "Money won't make you happy."

Author and speaker John Ortberg told a great Monopoly story. He said his grandma "was a master of the board." They had fun, but he always felt he could never get an edge. She knew something he didn't, and he always left the loser. Every time she won, she would finish by saying, "Son, someday you'll learn to play the game."

One summer he played Monopoly with his next-door neighbor every day for hours and, in his words, he "learned to play the game." He learned how to trade and be ruthless with his competitors. He learned that he should buy almost everything he landed on. He learned the game was about total acquisition. The game was about having everything by hook or crook. Finally, he had become a master of the game.

When the time came for him to play his grandma again, he was ready. And at the final showdown, he won. He took everything she had. He took her properties, her houses and hotels, and he took all that glorious money. As he glowed in his victory, she said to him, "Well done! You've mastered the game. You've acquired everything. Now it's time for your second lesson: it all goes back in the box."

This was not what he wanted to hear. He didn't want it to all go back in the box.

His grandma turned to him and said, "John, this game has been around a long time. It was here before you were born, and it will be here long after you've gone. So take all those titles, all those buildings, and all that money, and put it back in the box."

Naturally, Ortberg asked his audience how long they would play the game of acquisition before they realized it's not enough. In the end, even if you "get the ultimate house, the ultimate purchase, total financial security, and the thrill wears off (and it will wear off), then what?" He said, "Players come and players go, but it all goes back in the box. Houses and cars, titles and clothes, filled barns, bulging portfolios, even your body will all go back in the box." Too many people realize this only when it's too late.

Don't let it get you down. There's nothing wrong with money. The main point is that first things need to be first, and second things need to be second. Your relationship with God and others needs to be at the top of your list. Making money and succeeding is number two. When God, family, and friendships are first in your life (in that order), you will over time have way more joy and energy.

Dallas Willard gave us the ultimate test when he said to pray the prayer, "God, don't give me more money than my character can handle."

If you can't pray that prayer in earnest, you're in good company. The last thing most people want to do is hint to God in any way that they don't want money. The first time I asked our church to say this together in a service, the congregational words came out garbled and unenthusiastic, followed by chuckles as people realized how little they wanted to say it. On the other hand, if you are one of those rare souls who really cares more about your character than your income, if you recognize the trap of money, then you're ready to receive financial blessing from God. The more you can pray that prayer with real heart, the more money I hope God gives you, because the money will likely be from God and not from greed, and it will help a lot of people.

> You will actually be more successful in your work and finances if work and finances take second place.

The interesting thing is in the long run, you will actually be more successful in your work and finances if work and finances take second place. Friends will help you. Your family will support you. God will pour out opportunity on your life and give you favor. Most of all, you'll have everything you need to live a life of meaning and significance. You'll endure whatever financial loss you face because it won't be absolutely connected to your identity.

God Treasures You

Everyone worships something, even atheists and agnostics. Worship means you treasure something even more than yourself. You talk about it. Think about it. You write songs about it. You build rites, ceremony, culture, and taboos around it. All your passion, or spiritual energy, is focused toward that one treasured thing, above all else. Some people worship sports teams; others worship their political party. Most people are polytheistic in their worship, meaning they have many "gods." Though we often think idols are from the past or third-world countries, the West is just as idolatrous as the rest of the world, and that's normal and ordinary.

What's extraordinary is to abandon idols and put your faith in one God alone—to value him above all and to trust him even when things don't go your way. That's amazing. When a human being focuses on God alone, worships him, and trains his or her life according to his will, that person inherits an amazing life.

Worshiping God alone elevates culture. The greatest art and music in history came from people using their craft to glorify God. Michelangelo's *David*, *Pieta*, and Sistine Chapel and da Vinci's *The Last Supper* are widely recognized as the greatest pieces of art on earth. Bach's "Jesu, Joy of Man's Desiring" and Handel's *Messiah* are among the greatest pieces of music ever written. They are Christian and elevate the heart and mind to heaven. Art, music, and culture, when birthed out of monotheism, dignify existence.

There is certainly great secular music and art today, as well, and I'm thankful for it. But on the whole, it will not be timeless. Even when it lifts the soul, secular art often lacks the soul to actually do what it is attempting.

I believe that by far the greatest art of today is architecture, and if you ask an architect what his dream building is to design, he will tell you it's a cathedral. When God is at the center of our culture, it lifts hearts and minds to the heavens. When he is not, it degenerates us into animals.

By no means am I neglecting the many problems of our religious past, especially in the areas of science and liberal education, but even the greatest scientists had a religious bent. Einstein believed in a pantheist god, Newton wrote a systematic theology, and a Belgian priest discovered the Big Bang theory. His name was Georges Lemaître and early on, his theory of the origin of the universe was highly criticized by atheists for being "overtly creationistic."

When we build a culture that worships God and his core attributes of truth, goodness, and beauty, he lifts up his people to glory. When we abandon God for the things he made, we wallow in the dust. Humans are found teetering somewhere between animals and angels. What we worship will tip the balance. Monotheism elevates the soul to the angels and paganism turns people into animals. Whether it's worshiping a literal idol or a Ferrari, people lose their humanness if they lose sight of the Lord.

You are God's treasure. You are not what you have. Much of life is a journey of letting go. Jobs will come and go. Money will come and go. Opportunity missed or seized will come and go. But in the end you belong to him. In the end that will be all that matters. God longs to be with you. Even now he longs to spend time with you and hear the sound of your voice. He is jealous for you. (That's basically the opening line of David Crowder's worship song "How He Loves.") It breaks God's heart to see us desire material things that are dead more than we desire him, the one who is the Source of all life and joy.

By no means do I intend to diminish the awesomeness of God by painting him to be weak or confused in some way. Rather, if in all his power, wrath, and joy, this limitless, timeless, changeless Creator, larger than the scope of the whole universe, has his heart and mind set on you, why do you have your heart and mind set on an Audi? There is so much to be gained in a deep, abiding relationship with God that it makes all else seem like tripe. When you drink in the love of God, you'll be so satisfied you'll say, "Take the whole world. I turn my back on its pleasures, allures, devices, and treasures. Give me Jesus."

The irony is this kind of person, whose eyes are fixed on God and little else, opens up her whole existence to such an incredible outpouring of real material blessing from heaven. The less we desire and hold on to success, the more he will entrust it to us. As we move from being owners of our stuff to managers (meaning it all belongs to God for his purposes and is only temporarily in our control), God often releases more into our lives. We have no right or reason to define how this will look, or when it will take shape, but we can trust that the one who holds the cattle on a thousand hills is willing and able to provide. Jesus taught:

> So do not worry, saying, "What shall we eat?" or "What shall we drink?" or "What shall we wear?" For the pagans run after all these things, and your heavenly Father knows that you need them. But seek first his kingdom and his righteousness, and all these things will be given to you as well. (Matt. 6: 31–33)

That's the Word of God. It's a promise. Put God first, and he'll put you first.

Generosity Is the Antidote

Generosity without a need for recognition is a great practice. It's called the *discipline of secrecy*. It's also the best way to invite God's blessing into your material pursuits. When you give to those in need, whether or not the person is grateful, you show God that the money is his and not yours. Generosity is the best way to train yourself into finding an identity in something other than material possessions.

Whether it's your money, your words, your time, or your attention, being generous with people who need you invites blessing into your life.

When you bless others, you'll be blessed. When you withhold blessing, blessing will be withheld from you. The Bible says, "I will bless those who bless you, and the one who curses you I will curse" (Gen. 12:3 NASB). I read that years ago and began thinking; *That was written for everyone in covenant with God, not just me.* If I bless or curse others, I will also invite it on myself.

I call this the *conduit theory.* You are a conduit for heaven or hell, blessing or cursing, and as they pass through you, they get on you. You can't paint a house red without getting a little paint on yourself. You can't bless others without getting a little blessing on you. You also can't curse others without getting a little on you. That's why people who are always saying the worst about others seem to also have the worst luck. As they spew nastiness on others, a little gets on them, in the spiritual sense. That's why being positive and generous, even when you're angry and tired, keeps you in a better place in life. You are setting up for yourself a good future, because you are sowing the seeds that will prosper you and not harm you.

When we find our identity in what we own, we become misers, and we eat our seed instead of planting it in the ground. When we let go of an identity in our material belongings, we free ourselves to plant seed in the soil that will reap a lasting harvest. God wants you to be blessed, but first you have to stop trusting in the world and start trusting in him. Continue to be a positive, faith-filled, and generous person. It will reap dividends in your future.

Jesus taught his disciples, "Do not store up for yourselves treasures on earth, where moth and rust destroy, and where thieves break in and steal. But store up for yourselves treasures in heaven, where neither moth nor rust destroys, and where thieves do not break in and steal" (Matt. 6:19–20 NASB). As a child growing up, I pictured treasure in heaven as legitimate, real, pirate-style treasure. I thought when I got to heaven, I would have a treasure vault filled with pearls, gems, and gold coins that were the sum total of all my good works. To be honest, this was not appealing to me as a kid, because I wanted this kind of treasure while still on earth.

Treasure in heaven does not look this way. In fact, the treasure you've stored up in heaven is made available to you now. It's much like an ATM. You may have treasure in your bank account in your hometown, but when you travel overseas, you can still access your deposits from an ATM. In the same way, when you live according to Jesus' way, you are storing up for yourself treasures in heaven that will pay off in ways much bigger than money.

Treasures in Heaven Are Available Now!

In the Bible the word *heaven* is always plural. It should read "the heavens," but most Bibles erroneously translate it as singular. This is a big mistake because we miss out on the fullest understanding of heaven. The highest level of heaven is where you go when you die if you've trusted your life to Christ. But heaven is also present with every believer who is living in "the range of God's effective will," as Dallas Willard put it. In other words, if you know and love God, you are already experiencing the lowest level of heaven today and have access to its treasure. Wherever God is, heaven is. So when you do the things that store up treasures in heaven, you will be storing up something you can access and will have forever, both now and when you die.

This is one of the main points of the Sermon on the Mount. Years ago, I decided I wanted to truly understand and know this sermon. I memorized it. I translated it from Greek to English. In that process the greatest surprise that no theologian seems to mention is how often Jesus talked about reward. He kept rhetorically asking, "What reward will you get?" I realized the reward he was talking about was treasure in heaven.

I often think of treasure in heaven as a culmination of knowledge, godly joy and peace, and a lot of what the world would erroneously call good karma. In short, it's the promise of the good life. It's verve and energy.

When your life is fixed on knowing God and others deeply, you are making a huge investment in heaven. This is a reward that will not fade or tarnish. You are investing in a life full of joy and emotional energy. When you spend your life doing good and not evil, you will firmly establish your identity in dignity and not in hidden shame. When you live to please God and not people, you rid your life of many of the fears of rejection and abandonment. You'll sleep better. When you ask God for wisdom instead of wealth, as King Solomon did, you will likely get both. These things are like a spiritual portfolio that in the end will often lead to material abundance. But these heavenly treasures are richer and better in the sense that they give what you thought you would get from money: treasures from heaven will give you freedom. Storing up treasures in heaven is laying the foundation for an unworried and joyful life in God's kingdom.

Stop trying to prove yourself through your possessions. Instead, store up for yourself treasures in heaven, because these never go back in the box. Let go of the acquisition of material things as a way of proving yourself to others. If you like something or want something, get it and enjoy it. But don't make it so important that it has any effect on how you think people view you or how you view yourself. You are not what you have. You are who has you, and he will never let go.

7

YOU'RE NOT WHAT YOU HAVE—BUT GRATITUDE WILL GIVE YOU MORE

> If the only prayer you said was thank
> you, that would be enough.
> —Meister Eckhart

Southern California and the greater Los Angeles area is one of the wealthiest places on earth. Every day you see beautiful people wearing the latest designer clothes, drinking expensive coffee, and sending their children to the finest schools and extra-curricular activities. (You mean your school doesn't have a lacrosse, surf, or golf team?) On the surface, everyone here has an almost perfect life, the kind most people would dream of. But having lived and served here for a long time, I know they are anything but. Though they are wealthy, these people are also in debt, stressed out, out of energy, and still hungry for more. In a way, Californians are an extreme version of everyone else. Most people who live here moved here.

I don't say this to be critical of my people. I love them and love

California. I say it because I've realized that, in Fyodor Dostoevsky's words, "Man is a creature who can get used to anything." Though many people here are rich, they are as hungry as the rest of us—maybe hungrier. It seems that in life, sufficiency has as much to do with the heart as it does the bank account. If you can't be happy with what you have, you likely won't be happy when you have a lot.

Hustling

Living for many people is like chasing the oasis in the distance. Elusive yet still in sight, it teases us as we trudge through the desert thinking, *I'm almost there.* Exhausted, thirsty, we keep "hustling for worthiness," as Brené Brown put it. The reasoning is, *Just a little more, then I'll spend more time doing what I love, then I'll focus on my relationships, then I'll pray more.* But then we never get there. Or perhaps we get to the oasis and it's not enough. So we trudge through more sand and heat in search of more.

Notice I said "we." Pastors struggle with needing to be loved and appreciated just like everyone else. In fact, we can often be self-absorbed and ego driven and bend the truth about attendance numbers or how we're feeling emotionally. There's a reason so many preachers' kids leave the faith. For pastors, the day that is Sabbath rest for everyone else becomes the hardest day of work of the whole week. Our families can be dysfunctional and feel farthest from God on Sunday because pastors are busy hustling for worthiness from their congregations. We have the same need for approval and meaning as everyone else. This need is inescapable if we don't learn to rest and let go in the love of God.

Scarcity

Almost every night before I go to bed, I do the alarm-clock math. As I set my alarm for the next day, I instantly measure how much sleep I'm going to get. As I measure, I'm keenly aware of the fact it won't be as much as I would have liked. I'll find a way to get up a little later, but it's only a consolation. I'm going to be tired tomorrow. There's this irritating sense that I'm going to be playing catchup . . . again. This touches on my deep sense of tiredness and reinforces the belief that my life is somehow scarce.

I love Lynne Twist's reflection on this. She wrote:

> For me, and for many of us, our first waking thought of the day is "I didn't get enough sleep." The next one is "I don't have enough time." Whether true or not, that thought of not enough occurs to us automatically before we even think to question or examine it. We spend most of the hours and the days of our lives hearing, explaining, complaining, or worrying about what we don't have enough of. Before we even sit up in bed, before our feet touch the floor, we're already inadequate, already behind, already losing, already lacking something. And by the time we go to bed at night, our minds are racing with a litany of what we didn't get, or didn't get done, that day. We go to sleep burdened by those thoughts and wake up to that reverie of lack . . . This internal condition of scarcity, this mind-set of scarcity, lives at the very heart of our jealousies, our greed, our prejudice, and our arguments with life.[1]

Money has little bearing on whether or not a person feels they have enough and are enough. We always compare up, not down. We look at those who are better looking, wealthier, more liked, more popular, and more often promoted. We don't compare ourselves to those who can't hold down a job and don't meet up to the world's standards of beauty. There will always be another hill to conquer unless we can be at peace with who we are and where we are.

Years ago, I went to business school before I followed the prompting to serve God in pastoral ministry. I wanted to be rich. I read books on investing and becoming financially free and read my *Wall Street Journal* every morning. As I was finishing up school, I began working and interning at an investment firm. Many of these business people were working eighty-hour weeks, some with sofas that functioned as beds in their offices. They made incredible amounts of money, but had no time to spend it. Many were alcoholics.

Around that time I had the incredible opportunity to sit with a business titan—a billionaire who started his life in poverty. He's an incredible person, with a deep love for people and life, who has given millions of dollars away to charity, and he has a terrific reputation in the business world. He's lived the kind of life books are written about. His legacy will go on for generations. As we sat in one of his many mansions talking casually, he said to me, "Bobby, you know I never really made it in business. It's like I got into the NBA, but I'm just a bench warmer. I'm not Michael Jordan." He was serious. He was sad about his self-perceived lack of accomplishment. This man who'd accomplished so much was still hustling for worthiness.

After that conversation, I decided to trust in the wisdom of Jesus Christ and not to worry about money or about proving myself. I wanted financial freedom, but not at the cost of joy today. I made a decision to walk a new path: to be a pastor.

But the temptations of insufficiency are not just in the secular vocations. They are everywhere because they are within. Today, I'm daily handing my imperfections to God and trusting he will provide me with everything I need exactly when I need it. I'm learning to walk by faith, with my hands and my heart open, trusting, not holding on or hustling.

Open Hands

When we look at our hands, we often see a reflection of our heart. With our hands we work, we give, and we bless. With our hands we hang on to things tightly or let them go. The open hand is the symbol of holding things, but holding them loosely. We support what's in the open hand, but we don't cling to it. The open hand is the posture of both giving and receiving. With an open hand, we embrace a hurting friend. With an open hand we drink from a river or receive the Eucharist.

When we hang on to things too tightly, our hands become clinched fists. We fight with closed hands. We control. We manipulate our destiny. The clinched-fisted heart is the one that tries to manufacture the perfect outcome. It doesn't ever open or let go and therefore cannot receive the good things that God has. Like a locked door, nothing good or bad may enter.

I've begun to see my life in this manner: that I'm either living with open hands or clinched fists. I'm learning to live my life with an open hand, the posture of a trusting heart. With the open hand I reach toward heaven, that my loving Father would take a hold of it. I hope, as a child would, that he will guide me through the fog of life to a destiny of his choosing. I've learned to stop beating against the waves, to stop hurrying and making things happen, and instead live every day with gratitude and trust, at peace with who I am, going with the flow of the river of life. Though bumpy at times, this river only leads to good places.

All you need to do is look at a child to see you don't need wealth to be happy. Even the poorest children only need a square meal and a friend to enjoy life to the fullest. Children know "the best toys aren't toys," as my friend Bill says. Sticks become swords, trashcan lids become shields, boulders become ogres to slay, and trees become giants to aid us.

The suffering of life—rejection, abuse, and loss—move us from the easygoing life of childhood to the stresses of adulthood. But in the end we have the choice to live every day with joy in spite of what we don't have. The way we do this is by practicing gratitude.

Spontaneous Joy

I find it strange that nearly everyone from every culture, both young and old, has the same spontaneous reaction when they are super excited about something. With an open-mouthed shout and wide eyes, both hands shoot into the air and the whole body stretches heavenward. You see it from fans in sports, from someone being called to "come on down" on *The Price is Right*, and in the way NASA engineers rejoiced when endangered astronauts landed safely in Houston. It's the expression of elation—joy, gratitude, and excitement mixed together.

Incidentally, this open-handed, elated gesture is the same motion many Christians make in times of deep worship. It, too, is almost always spontaneous, like when a congregational song reaches its climax and an amazing tune or heart-gripping lyrics cause everyone to raise his or her hands in the air to a loving God. If you're standing in the back of the church and you see this happen, you can almost imagine you are looking at many little children asking for their parent to pick them up. This is truly the heart of the life of the open hand. Worship, joy, and gratitude are nearly all the same thing.

Being grateful naturally points the heart heavenward and will always be a kind of worship. Worship means acknowledging the good that is and thanking God for making it so. This is why author and theologian G. K. Chesterton said, "The worst moment for an atheist is when he feels a profound sense of gratitude and has no one to thank." Being a grateful person will always make you a better person. It will cause you to think about ultimate reality and will relax you. When you are grateful, you focus not on what you have lost, but simply what you have left, and believe you can have more. Grateful people are happy people. That's why it's impossible to picture a very grateful person who is also depressed or angry.

Nurturing Positivity

We need to nurture a positive heart in a negative world, and that's not easy to do. Though society may portray it as unintellectual or Pollyanna-ish, being positive and grateful is hard work. Being negative is the easy way to go, and it's the default for most people. Being grateful is divine at its core. It requires effort, because being grateful isn't just a feeling. It's a choice.

Society itself works daily to train us toward negativity, to be afraid. Bad news sells, and most people have an unrealistic view of the world, because no one reports good news—and even if they did, no one would read it. Author and speaker Shawn Achor called this "medical-school syndrome." He said, tongue in cheek, "As first-year medical school students read through all of the symptoms and diseases that could happen, [they] realize [they] have all of them." He said his brother-in-law, who was in his first year of medical school at Yale, called him and said, "Shawn, I have leprosy." Achor then said he had no idea how to console his brother-in-law because he had just gotten over an entire week of menopause.

Achor said that as we read and watch the news, we begin to have medical-school syndrome, where we believe journalists' portrayals are the "accurate accounting of the ratio of positive versus negative in the world." Bad news causes ratings to go up, and our outlook of the world goes down.[2]

> Being grateful naturally points the heart heavenward and will always be a kind of worship.

Recently I've taken a break from the news altogether. I've stopped watching it on TV or reading it online and stopped going on Twitter. It's been about six weeks now, and I'm not sure if I'm ever going back. I've decided to listen to music instead.

Put into the rhythms of your life the daily practice of gratitude. Say thank you to God, and say it to people. Write about it. Take pictures of the things you're grateful for. Make it your first thought in the morning and your last words before you go to bed. Let "thank you" be the last words at your death. That's what Dallas Willard did. As you put into practice daily rhythms of gratitude, you will feel your muscles and posture toward life becoming more relaxed. You'll smile more and maybe, hopefully, become the annoyingly happy person that people mock because they just can't believe it's real.

By living every day in a spirit of relaxed gratitude, you are setting up for yourself a fantastic future. Grateful people become magnets for miracles. They attract blessings from God and others.

Grateful Children

I love doting on my children when they are grateful. In the same way God loves doting on you when you are grateful. I remember my daughter was once playing the free version of the *My Little Pony* app on my phone. She finally got to the part where she had to pay one dollar to open up the next level. She begged me to buy it. Looking at it, I saw they had a deal: buy one land for one dollar or all fifteen for three dollars. I thought to myself, *I don't want to lose money*, and bought all fifteen.

You would have thought my daughter had just won the lottery. She threw her hands in the air, jumped up and down, and started kissing me so much it was almost annoying. Almost. I thought to myself, *I hope she doesn't always act this grateful for everything or I'll be broke. I'll give her everything!*

I think God feels and responds the same way with us. As we thank him, even for the smallest things, he opens heaven even more. Thankful people are setting up for themselves such a fantastic future.

It's just the opposite for thankless people. No one wants to keep giving gifts to those who aren't grateful. This is why entitlement destroys joy. The thankless person is a hurtful person. The one who gives feels taken advantage of, and the one who receives just gets what he or she expected. The more you thank God and others, the deeper you'll connect with them, the more they will help you, and the more joy and energy you'll have in general.

Gratitude Is Productive

Grateful people get results. They get results from their colleagues, from their bosses, and from their employees. Grateful people are in a flow of joy and energy and naturally attract others to themselves. These types of appreciative people have no problem thanking others for what they're "supposed to do." When you thank people for what they're already supposed to be doing, you give them energy and drive to go the extra mile. You are not simply telling them, "Because I'm thanking you, I'm acknowledging this was not in your realm of responsibility." That's what we're afraid of, as though thanking your husband for taking out the trash means he doesn't have to do it anymore. If you thank your husband for taking out the trash, I promise you he will do it more, not less. People want to matter. They want to know that even though they were supposed to do it, you noticed and appreciated them.

We should be genuine when we need to have difficult conversations with the people we do life with. However, being perceived as a self-righteous, proud, or cynical critic by others is one of the worst things that can happen to you. Unlike the hopeful, energetic, thankful leaders previously mentioned, the self-righteous critic will push others away. They live constantly from a place of fear and self-pity. They want to be respected and taken seriously, but in the end, they are usually unadmired and lonely.

Judgmental people think they will get results by criticizing others. They will make jokes or do other things in passive-aggressive ways, hoping others will almost read their minds and deliver. This never gets long-term results and usually isolates the person, causing them to be more critical and embittered. What a trap. Don't get stuck in that rut. And if you do, start being humble, vulnerable, and thankful for the good your loved ones and colleagues have done, even if they were supposed to do it.

Become a Tourist in Your Own Town

Years ago, my wife and I fulfilled a lifelong dream to visit Paris. It was amazing. Long walks along the Seine, Notre Dame, art, shopping, lazy breaks with brie, baguettes, and chardonnay. It was heaven. While we were there, we looked at everything. We noticed every little thing— how the lamps had flowers, how the spaces between buildings were charmingly narrow, even little things like the fonts and colors used on public buildings and signs. Everything was photo worthy.

Coming home was the saddest. Paris was thousands of miles and dollars away. When would we see her again?

Walking around my supposedly boring hometown of Old Towne Orange, I came upon a group of Japanese tourists. They were pointing at a little Mickey Mouse engraved on the sidewalk I'd never noticed before. They were pointing at the buildings. Some movie they loved, *The Wonders*, had been filmed here in one of the old-town cafés, and of course they were taking pictures of everything. They didn't know me but wanted to take a picture with me as well, and in broken English my new Japanese tourist friends said how much they loved where I lived and how sad they were that soon they'd have to go back to boring old Japan.

All of a sudden I realized: everyone thinks they're from somewhere boring. When we are on vacation or traveling, we look at our surroundings in ways we never do when we are at home.

The rest of the day I decided to be a tourist in my own town, to see it the way my Japanese friends did. I had never really looked at the fountain in the middle of town. I put my hands in the cold water and looked at the ornate carving. I noticed how it made the air around it cooler. I was fascinated with the carved ceiling in the old roof at the bank. I even began paying closer attention to the many different types of people in my town I'd never noticed. I said to myself, "I live in a terrific place." My heart was filled with gratitude.

Practices of gratitude fill your heart with energy and vibrancy. If you put this book down and look to your spouse, your kids, or a friend nearby and say, "I don't say it enough: I'm just so grateful for you," you will feel a surge of energy. If their response is awkward, that's a surefire sign they are not used to being thanked by you. It's a gratitude deficit. Don't worry about that. It just means you now have a practical way to improve your life and theirs.

As I mentioned earlier in the book, one scientific study asked people to write a letter of thanks to someone they care about and then read that letter to that person aloud. They asked that people make it real and not a joke. The study, which measured happiness, showed the reader had a jump in overall happiness that lasted, on average, more than a month. Another study on happiness by Robert Emmons showed that writing down things you're grateful for was the only nonmedical way you could permanently increase your overall sense of happiness.[3]

It's important to know, "I'm not what I have." Even more, our self-talk needs to be, "I'm so grateful for what I have." The more grateful you are for what you have, the more you will get out of life, and the more joy you will have from those things. Gratitude trains you into the life of the open hand. When we live every day with gratitude, we train our identity away from insufficiency and into knowing we already have everything we need. We go from scarcity to fullness.

YOU'RE NOT WHAT OTHERS SAY ABOUT YOU

To avoid criticism, say nothing, do nothing, be nothing.
—Elbert Hubbard

Have you ever thought about the power of a word? Look around. Everything that exists is so because someone said something. Every building you've ever seen is there because at one point someone pointed at the spot and said, "Build it." Every war exists because someone said something like, "Attack." The greatest speeches in the world find a place in our history because they defined or even started great movements, for good or evil. All the power in the universe originates with words.

God spoke the universe into being with words. John describes the creation story in this way: "In the beginning was the Word, and the Word was with God, and the Word was God . . . The Word became flesh and made his dwelling among us" (John 1:1, 14). Quite literally, Jesus is the Word of God among us. The words you hear change your life and the words you say change your life. It's that simple.

Spoken Words

I've always believed prayers have more power when spoken aloud. There's concreteness to saying it out loud. Saying your prayers out loud somehow makes it more real. You can be caught doing it. Your physical ears hear the sound of the prayer. Your physical body is touched. Passersby will hear it too.

With words we bless. With words we curse. Ancient pagan cultures would do things like gag witches or cut out their tongues, believing they were taking away their power to do magic. If they couldn't speak, they couldn't curse. In Greece they would pay sophists to give speeches. Throughout history people have paid priests, witch doctors, and sages to speak a blessing over them. In the Bible King Balak of Moab paid the diviner Balaam to speak a curse over the Hebrew people. God intervened and wouldn't let him (Num. 22). Apparently, Balaam had some power in his words as well. And I don't know about you, but I have more than once put the Bible on audio or listened to worship music when I was scared at home. Those words effect real change.

All of this to say it's a big deal when someone, anyone, says something over you—a compliment or affirmation of your good work.

Other words can create a permanent splinter in your mind by offending you. I still have memories of complete strangers saying awful things to me. Those words kept me up for a couple of nights. I didn't know those people. I certainly didn't like them or respect them. Yet even today, they still have a place in my memory, just because of words.

One of the goals of the Creed of the Beloved is to get rid of the words the world says to us and embrace the words our loving Father speaks over us. No word is more powerful than his. His word is final and it is good.

In the end, it's all about identity (how you view yourself) and which words you will believe (what words you put your faith in). Your identity is likely constructed by the words you've heard your whole life. Perhaps when you were a kid, you were bullied at school. Maybe one or both of your parents were in the habit of being playfully mean. Though they would laugh when they called you a screw-up, you took it to heart. All of us in our childhood heard discouraging words from family, friends, enemies, teachers, and even magazines and TV that reinforced a view of ourselves that we are simply not enough. Because of these words, we feel we are not thin enough, smart enough, lucky enough, or wanted enough.

Mocking, insulting, or judgmental words can cause our already fragile souls to become brittle. When someone says something offensive or mean spirited or gossips or lies about us, it can feel like the final blow. If someone says something kind, we believe they may be making it up to be nice or simply filling the space in a conversation. But if someone criticizes us, we absolutely believe it. After all, who would lie about *not* liking your work?

Throughout life you will hear both negative and positive words said about you. You will hear them from the world, and you will hear them from God. Though every word you hear will likely affect you in some way, you can choose which words to believe. This belief is called *faith*. Faith is the thing that gives words power. You can have faith in the word of God, or you can have faith in what people say about you. You typically cannot believe both.

> You are not what others say about you. You are what God says about you. You are beloved.

Have faith in the Word of God. When others say hurtful things about you, God is blessing you. When others remind you of your past, God reminds you of your future—that it's blessed, joyful, and abundant. You are not what others say about you. You are what God says about you. You are beloved.

Don't meditate on the negative. When we dwell on the nasty and critical things people say about us, the words take root and have power over us. When we repeat those words over ourselves by saying something like, "Oh, sorry, I'm so stupid," the negative seeds of yesterday begin bearing bad fruit in our lives. But when we meditate on the Bible and the Word of God in our hearts, we form a new identity. Believe what God says over you and not what the world says.

Often our spiritual batteries are empty because we dwell on what others say about us, good or bad. There are times when others say something great about us, and though it's nice and feels good, it can easily tempt us into people pleasing and pretending. God wants us to let go of what others say about us and believe what he's saying over us. Until we hear the voice of God, believe it, and act in faith according to it, we will lack power to be the kind of people God has called us to be.

This is what makes Christianity different: all other faiths say, "Do good and you will be good. Then, when you are good, you will belong. Keep being good and you will keep belonging. Don't bring shame to the faith." (Many churches and Christian denominations have echoed this same thing, but they are not teaching an orthodox view of the Christian faith. They are falling into the trap of the Pelagian heresy, which teaches you are saved by works.) Jesus said, "Come into the house a broken, ragamuffin sinner, and you will belong." You belong not because of your great reputation or good works but simply because Christ died for you and will raise you up. Die to any identity found in the world, and embrace the identity given to you through God in Christ Jesus.

Though most big religions have a similar goal to Christianity (Make people good.), Christianity says God does the changing by grace through faith. As you believe new words spoken over you by a loving Father, those things will become so.

Beloved (Jesus)

The Gospels say that Jesus' identity was affirmed in his baptism before he began his public ministry. Before Jesus did anything noteworthy, he was baptized, and the heavens opened up. The voice of the Father spoke over him, "This is My beloved Son, in whom I am well-pleased" (Matt. 3:17

NASB). He hadn't really accomplished anything yet. As far as we know he hadn't preached much; he hadn't saved or healed anyone. Still the Father said, "I'm pleased in him!" The Father's affirmation was not about the merits or accomplishments of Jesus, but about how he loved the son just as he was, the way any father adores a child.

This is what God is saying over you. In spite of your imperfections, and despite the fact you may not have accomplished much, God is pleased in you, as a Father is pleased in his child.

After his baptism, Jesus was brought into the desert to be tested. There, as he fasted for forty days, the Devil came and challenged him in three ways (see Matt. 4:1–11):

- "Turn these rocks into bread," he said in the desert. This was the challenge that Jesus didn't have enough.
- "Jump off this tower, and the angels will catch you," he said at the temple. "Then all your peers and enemies will see you really are the Son of God." This was the temptation to glory.
- "Bow down to me and worship me, and I'll give you back the whole world," he finally said. This was the temptation to hurry to the destiny without paying the price.

I believe Jesus really did struggle with these temptations. Yet in every case he responded with the written Word of God. He would say, "It is written . . ." and essentially throw the Bible at his adversary. Christ carried the words, "You are My beloved Son, in whom I am well-pleased," in every dark moment of his ministry. He put his faith in the identity of being the beloved, and that sustained him.

You, Too, Are Blessed

God the Father says the same thing over you. You are his beloved child in whom he is well-pleased. God the Father loves you as much as he loves

Jesus his son. If not, he wouldn't have sent Jesus to the cross for you. This is why John declared, "Behold what manner of love the Father has given to us, that we should be called children of God. And that is what we are!" (1 John 3:1 BSB).

If you believe it, you will have power to withstand any trial and temptation. Having joy and energy in life is about living from a relaxed place of trusting his words and not the words of the world. You are not who others say you are. You are what God says. You are his beloved child.

People-Pleasing Trap

Living a life that pleases God is much better than living a life that pleases people. As Billy Graham said, "Our society strives to avoid any possibility of offending anyone—except God." Pleasing people exhausts you. Doing your best to always make sure everyone else is happy at your own expense is not healthy. It will totally drain your life of the energy and vision you need to move forward to your next calling.

That aside, you will also often find yourself pretending to endorse things you don't honestly approve of because you don't want to have an awkward encounter. You'll find yourself wasting time you could have spent on personal growth or with God because you allow people to violate your boundaries. Often at the heart of this behavior is the fear of what people will think or say about you.

Don't be rude or offensive, but always be you, just as you are. Think about how to lead a life pleasing to God as his beloved child. When we think of how God thinks about us instead of how people think about us, we are given the gift of being filled with spiritual energy. Here we find the perfect balance between serving and loving people, while still maintaining our principles and boundaries.

Jesus warned us about the dangers of having the kind of reputation where only good things are said about you all the time: "Woe to you when everyone speaks well of you, for that is how their ancestors treated the false prophets" (Luke 6:26). He also said:

> Blessed are you when people hate you, when they exclude you and insult you and reject your name as evil, because of the Son of Man. Rejoice in that day and leap for joy, because great is your reward in heaven. For that is how their ancestors treated the prophets. (Luke 6:22–23)

It's clear to me that if I am living life in the kingdom of God with Jesus, I will often be at odds with society. I will believe things society doesn't believe. I will do things they don't do. I will reject things they love. This does not lead to being the most popular kid in school. It leads to being bullied, mocked, and rejected by many. If I love God, truly love people, don't agree with everyone all the time, and live differently, there will be some people who hate my guts, and that's okay. In fact, it's better than okay. There's a reward for that.

Aside from the reward of just honoring God and doing what is morally right, there is the additional reward of freedom from managing my reputation. Reputation management drains your spiritual batteries more than almost anything. You can't write what you want to write, paint what you want to paint, sing what you want to sing, or do what you want to do. Managing one's reputation is slavery to the mundane. It guarantees that you will be both exhausted and uncreative. You will find no freedom in it because you will draw the neediest, most judgmental people to you, and you will enter a kind of enabling relationship with them.

Say what God has called you to say. Do what God has called you to do. Be who he has called you to be. A life pleasing to God leads to a life of freedom. Be as kind and loving as possible, but don't feel like you have to placate everyone. Forget about it. Follow Jesus and be free.

C. S. Lewis said that everyone who met Jesus was compelled to love and worship him or was driven to hate him with an almost mad desire to kill him. I think something similar happens to us the more we as his followers become like him. Yes, some people say they "like Jesus but not

Christians," but honestly, I'm not sure they have a clear picture of the One who spoke truth to power, called sinners to live righteously, kicked over the moneychangers' tables, and drew a crystal-clear line between heaven and hell. As you grow to be more like Christ, many people will admire you and want to learn from you, and others will dislike or hate you. The more you are like Jesus, the more polarizing you will become. If you've never been criticized for your faith, you are still a "baby Christian." If you don't have any critics, you are not doing anything different than the rest of the world. If you don't have any competitors or enemies, then stand out in your faith and you'll get some. You'll find freedom in saying no and living differently from everyone else. The life of the chameleon is not for you. You are a lion.

Whether you've been criticized for your faith or condemned for being a dreamer or an outsider challenging the status quo, criticism will always be there, and it will only grow. Why don't you think there are more challengers, dreamers, and people of faith? Because dealing with the onslaught of criticism is taxing.

Haters Gonna Hate = Training

When we started our church plant "The Gathering," we did some pretty innovative stuff for the time. We'd receive criticism, and it was hard, but it would rarely keep me up at night, because it was petty. I usually moved on. Later, when I came to lead the very large and televised Shepherd's Grove, I inherited what felt like a total bombardment of constant criticism. People on Facebook and YouTube were calling me "green" or "just another fake religious guy out to get your money." Others called me a "heretic." Somehow, some folks saw me as too conservative while others saw me as too liberal. Someone even put together a whole website dedicated to criticizing and gossiping about me. I was not ready for that and would regularly reply, feeling angry, judged, and totally misunderstood.

One day on a "date day" with Hannah, we walked around Universal City Walk in LA. My mind was heavy with all the mostly unfair criticism

I was getting. I wish you could hear the whiny self-talk that was going on in my head. Then I saw this kid with a big black baggy shirt that said in bold white letters, "If you ain't got haters, you ain't doin' s***."

It was a revelation. I saw something profound in the profane. Somehow God used this kid and his shirt to speak to me.

"It's training," I felt the Lord say to me later. "All that criticism, especially the fake stuff, is training." If I wanted to do the big things for God, I would have a lot of critics. If I wanted to go where he'd called me to go, this would just be training. It was going to be much harder when I got there.

Changing the world is hard, because a lot of people like it just the way it is. But from that day I started thinking, *Man, I hope someday I have ten websites dedicated to criticizing me. I hope someday I have a cover story of a newspaper criticizing me. How great would that be?*

So in all things, put your faith in the voice of God, not the chaotic, hysterical, and critical words of society. Society is always in a constant state of anxiety. It needs you to lead it into peace, not follow it into the abyss. Sometimes people will love you. Other times they will hate you. Even worse, some will lie about you and gossip about your family. Let it go. God says you are loved.

If you are constantly halted by the cynicism of the world, you will not be as effective in your calling. The nasty words, gossip, and criticism of others will be the thing that most likely keeps you from your destiny. Very simply put, the more good you do, the more criticism you will get. Sometimes your ideas and speaking truth or goodness will be like opening the blinds on someone who is sleeping or hungover. They'll hate it. Sometimes the response will be jealousy. Sometimes guilt. In almost all cases, it's not your problem. Move forward.

Learning Not to Be Defensive

Yes, there are times when your friends and loved ones will legitimately criticize you, and this is when you really need to be rooted in your identity. Not so you can ignore it, but rather so you can hear it without being hurt or defensive. When the heart hinges on the approval of people, it becomes worn out. If this happens we can mistakenly think that a friend who challenges or criticizes us is now our enemy. In truth, one of the greatest gifts our friends can give us is to challenge and critique us while still loving us. They're helping us. As we listen to the voice of the beloved, wisdom or confrontation from our friends becomes a gift, not a threat. It has nothing to do with belonging.

As you grow in Christ you will actually long for your friends to be more honest with you. Because they know you best, they are well equipped to help you see your blind spots. This is wisdom. Proverbs 9:8–9 says:

> Do not rebuke mockers or they will hate you;
> rebuke the wise and they will love you.
> Instruct the wise and they will be wiser still;
> teach the righteous and they will add to their learning.

Or there's this great line from Ecclesiastes 7:5: "It is better to heed the rebuke of a wise person than to listen to the song of fools."

As we walk every day in the voice of the beloved, we receive a sort of inner constitution. People will see it. When we are galvanized by God's love, others know they can challenge us without hurting our friendship. That's great because it will put your Christian development into overdrive.

Loving Our Enemies

I often wonder how some people can be so destructive with their words, so reckless in the way they bring people down. People can be mean spirited or unfair in their criticism. Often it's petty gossip, lies, or people drudging up things from our past in order to hurt us. How do we then respond as Christians? Jesus teaches us to love and bless our enemies.

This teaching from Jesus is the most central to his ministry. It is also the least taught bit of wisdom in churches today. Too many pastors have not received training in this discipline and often struggle to reconcile it with their own behavior. As stated earlier, love doesn't mean you have warm feelings in your heart for your enemies. Rather, it means you care about them because they are children of God. The gift of loving our enemies sets us free from the world's game of dog-eat-dog retributive behavior. It allows us to simply say, "I'll just love everyone and let God sort them out later."

Viktor Frankl once said, "The one thing you can't take away from me is the way I choose to respond to what you do to me." That revelation, he claimed, saved his life. To paraphrase another of his quotes, the last of one's freedoms is to choose one's attitude in any given circumstance. Loving your enemies is one of the greatest ways you can prove you trust God with your life.

Letting Go of the Credit

Harry Truman said, "It's amazing what you can accomplish if you don't care who gets the credit." It can be galling when you work hard at something, it's your idea, and you do most of the work, and your boss takes the credit. This is another thing to let go of. When you stop caring about the praise of others and just work hard at doing what you love, the trend will keep going up even if there are little blips like this. You'll gain a much better reputation professionally by letting go of your reputation altogether. When you focus on a project or thing you love and don't care about who gets the credit, most people will give it to you in the long run. You'll become more valuable professionally, and people will notice.

Never take the credit of others. If you are a leader, give as much credit to your team as you can and take as much criticism personally, away from your team, as you can. You'll be more trusted and earn loyalty and respect from those following you.

So abandon the notion that anyone has any idea who you are. Most people don't. Don't let the words, good or bad, have any weight on your identity. Free yourself from that. Live every day in God's words. He says you are loved, he's proud of you, and he's going to get you where you need to go. Recharge your batteries by training your mind to forget about the negative stuff people say about you. Sleep better at night. Challenge people. Say "no" more. And find the freedom to do what you're supposed to do, no matter how crazy it may seem to others.

9

YOU'RE NOT WHAT
OTHERS SAY ABOUT YOU—
SO BE VULNERABLE

"What happens when people open their hearts?"
"They get better."
—Haruki Murakami, *Norwegian Wood*

Golden Eagle

In elementary school there was this system of merits called "golden eagles." Every time you did something good, like turning in your homework early or participating well in class, and a teacher noticed, you would be given a golden eagle. Collect ten of these and you would be honored in front of the whole school by being given the Golden Student Award.

I had my eye on the prize. I was going to get this award and show everyone what a terrific student I was. I cleaned up trash right where teachers could see me. I went out of my way to help and be nice to other students, especially when teachers were around. Pretty soon I started racking up the golden eagles. Victory was in sight.

One day during recess, I was throwing rocks against the wall to entertain myself. (Boys don't need a reason to do such things. If it's forceful and involves crashes or destruction, then it's fun.) Not paying attention, a teacher walked into my rock-throwing range. I nearly hit her and was given a sound shellacking and, of all things, a demerit. Now, a demerit meant you lost three golden eagles. But even worse, you had to get it signed off on by a parent. I worried all day.

My parents were divorced, and I lived with my dad. He was the stricter of my parents, and I knew he would not be pleased. I had no idea what he would do, but I didn't want to guess. My mom, however, who saw me on the weekends, was by default "the fun parent" and would have no problem signing my demerit. My plan was this: get Mom to sign it, hide it completely from Dad, then get thirteen golden eagles by working over-time on my goodness skills, and just pretend I'd gotten ten, and everyone goes home happy.

Little did I know that after you turn in the signed demerit, the school officials mail it back to you—for a keepsake, I guess.

I came home one day, and there he was—my dad, standing in my room, holding the demerit. He didn't have to say a word. I panicked. I didn't know what to do except cry. It wasn't just that he was there and he knew. I had been living a lie for days, and it was eating me up. I'd been constantly living in fear. I'd had nightmares that this scenario would happen, and now it had.

He simply said, "So you threw some rocks at a wall? Big deal. Why did you hide this from me?" He was much cooler than I'd thought he would be . . . and I instantly relaxed.

As children, we play these types of games with our parents, who either get really upset or just roll their eyes. I know my kids do it with me. But as adults, we can't play the game anymore. There's nothing worse in your marriage, friendships, or work environment than to be caught in a lie. If relationships are built on trust, getting caught in a lie says, "I don't trust you and you shouldn't trust me." Almost no lie is an island unto itself; it requires multiple lies to be maintained. We nervously watch this house of cards being built, hoping it will stand forever. It won't.

Masters of Deception

This concept is important. Most of us have become masters of deception in some form or another and are unable to connect deeply with others and have authentic, awesome emotional and spiritual energy. When I say we are "masters of deception," I don't mean we are all compulsive liars. But many of us deceive others by not being vulnerable, by exaggerating our condition, by withholding our heart, or by not sharing our opinion when it is needed. In these ways we treat our true self with contempt, managing our ego and showing only our best parts while hiding the parts we don't like. This mask—or the ideal self—we put forward, comes from a place of fear and keeps us shut up inside, unable to experience the freedom of God's love.

People really do lie . . . a lot. According to a recent study by the University of Massachusetts and Robert Feldman, people meeting for the first time will lie to one another an average of two to three times every ten minutes. These are not malicious lies, but little white lies that are used as "social lubricant" to either build oneself up ("I run ten miles every week to stay in shape" or "Sure, I love that book") or to keep from tearing the other person down ("I love your shoes. I wish I had a pair."). In the end we want to draw closer to people by making it less awkward, so we lie, and we usually don't even notice we're doing it.

Why do we lie so often when talking with someone we just met? Because we don't know that person well enough or because we don't trust him or her. *I lie to get this conversation moving along*, we tell ourselves. *Hopefully it will go well. After all, I don't want to come across as a weirdo.*

But growing in relationships with others requires a sort of stretching, trusting, and reaching out. It requires that we be vulnerable by sharing difficult things from our past, fears we bring into the friendship, losses or regrets that haven't quite healed. In vulnerable honesty we risk pushing people away, but without this honesty we remain unknown. One of the greatest joys a person can feel is to be seen deeply and still be liked. But it requires courage and means we must be at peace with the truth, even when we don't like it.

> One of the greatest joys a person can feel is to be seen deeply and still be liked.

We lie when we don't want to go out but don't want to hurt our friend's feelings. It's easier to say we already have plans than it is to tell them we're tired and just want to watch a movie at home alone. We lie when we don't want to face the consequences. We say, "It's going to be a huge mess, and I'm going to be in big trouble if they find out about this." We lie to cut corners, to get there faster, because after all, this process is taking too long.

Underneath all this lying is the fact that we are not at peace with the truth. This is not to say we don't want to know the truth, but rather we don't want others to know the truth about us. We are not at peace with who we are, inadequacies and all.

Maybe you are not at peace with your lack of education, so you hide it. Perhaps you are not at peace with your addiction, so you battle it alone. You are not at peace with your past and all your imperfections, so those stay hidden as well. But when you invite your dear friends, your family, and God into these realities, the painful truth begins to set you free.

Living at peace with the truth by allowing others to see it is scary and painful, but it liberates us. It's like setting a broken bone. It will hurt a lot, even more than breaking the bone, but it must happen to heal correctly. Telling the truth in your profession when others lie to get ahead can be painful, but it has to happen for you to live with joy. Confessing your sins or sharing your mistakes with others will relieve you of their burden.

Telling your spouse what you need even though it will make him or her angry will create an honest, shame-free relationship that is safe and full of spiritual energy.

Our desire to be good and our desire to be liked are always at odds with each other. All of us have a deep need to be good. It's absolute. That's why most bad people don't think they're bad; they think they're sort of neutral. The thief always blames the victim: "He shouldn't have left his wallet out. If I didn't take it, someone else would have."

Sometimes telling the truth and walking in the truth will mean you won't be liked. The problem is we want that too. But telling the truth to others might mean we hurt their feelings. We have to be at peace with that as well. Yes, we love people and sometimes decide to "take one for the team" or neglect our own desires or needs because "it's just not worth it." But then we start to feel secretly angry. It comes out in passive-aggressive ways, or we just withdraw by hiding or not responding. Well, this is hurtful too. In the end we have to get really good at telling truth in a way that is honest but still loving.

It's Core to Jesus' Life and Teaching

In the Sermon on the Mount, Jesus put forward the idea that we need to shoot straight—that our yes is always yes and our no is always no. Here's the actual text:

> You have heard that it was said to the people long ago, "Do not break your oath, but fulfill to the Lord the vows you have made." But I tell you, do not swear an oath at all: either by heaven, for it is God's throne; or by the earth, for it is his footstool; or by Jerusalem, for it is the city of the Great King. And do not swear by your head, for you cannot make even one hair white or black. All you need to say is simply "Yes" or "No"; anything beyond this comes from the evil one. (Matt. 5:33–37)

The original idea of oaths was to recognize God as a part of a transaction or conversation. It was originally ascribed in the Torah (the first five books of the Bible) for legal reasons but became a part of normal Jewish interaction. Eventually, dishonest people were able to use this rule to their advantage, like a religious loophole. It had become tradition that if you made an oath to the Lord, you were bound, but if you didn't make an oath, then you didn't have to do what you said you would do. Soon people started swearing by holy things, but not to the Lord himself, knowing the whole time what they were doing was dishonest. When the truth came out, they would respond, "Ah-ha! I swore by heaven but didn't swear to the Lord."

Truth in All Things

The goal is to train your tongue to speak only the truth in all things, even the little things. It's easier said than done. Often we say yes when we need to say no, or we lie instead of saying no, or we give half the truth, or we exaggerate. These modes of talking can become bad habits that wear down our spiritual battery. Aside from being immoral, they create unconscious feelings of guilt. In turn these half-truths and white lies stress us out because we have to remember what we've said so that we don't accidentally tell another lie. There's a Hawaiian proverb that describes this: "Never lie. It's too much to remember." All of that managing of deception takes a terrible toll on our bodies and minds.

You don't have to hide, deceive, exaggerate, or say yes all the time just to be liked. I encourage you to employ the ten-second rule. If you ever say something that isn't exactly true, you have about ten seconds to correct it and everyone's fine. Anything longer than that, and you'll face the awkward confession conversation. It looks like this: in a conversation you say, "Val Kilmer and I are really great friends." A few seconds go by, you know you've messed up, you see people wondering, and you correct yourself with, "Well, not great friends. I met him one time, and he signed my *Tombstone* DVD." (This exact scenario happened to me, by the way.) You smile sheepishly, everyone laughs it off, and you move on.

Look, no one is perfect and there will be many times when you feel pressure to think fast and resort to lying because you can't think of a good response quickly enough. Just employ the ten-second rule: "Sorry, I can't go because I have a doctor's appointment." Ten seconds go by and you follow-up with, "Actually, I don't have a doctor's appointment. I love you and love to see you, but I'm feeling tired and was really looking forward to having some time to myself." *Boom!* Not only did you not lie, but you were vulnerable to your friend about feeling tired and needing time to recharge, and now she feels closer to you. If she keeps pressuring you, just hold your ground. She'll live.

If people don't respect your boundaries when they are clearly set, they don't respect you. If you don't hold your boundaries when they are clearly set, you don't respect yourself. In order to live with joy and energy, you have to do the brave thing by maintaining boundaries and being honest. If people leave you because of those choices, they are probably not a good fit for your life. Trust me: life is better with friends who respect you and your boundaries. If you feel yourself constantly needing to lie or needing to people-please, something has gone awry. Remember, you're not what you do, what you have, or what others say about you. You don't have to deliver, you don't have to prove anything, and sometimes the healthy thing to do means disappointing people.

Extreme Vulnerability Leads to Extreme Joy

There are few things worse in this world than carrying the burden of a secret sin or a secret past. These secrets can drive things like addiction, a deep sense of shame, and constant worry that you'll be found out. Count it a joy if you've never had something like this. Most people do. One of my callings is to walk alongside people who are struggling with something hidden. It could be an affair, an addiction to prescription drugs or pornography, or something from their past they haven't shared with anyone. If I've learned anything from these conversations, it's that these shames, sins, and painful secrets (such as being abused as a child) have more power over your life when they remain hidden.

Most people can't stand the thought of the embarrassment or shame they may feel when the truth comes out. The idea of total vulnerability feels like, "My whole world will fall apart." Sometimes it does. But I can also tell you that anyone who has opened up about these secrets to their loved ones is always glad they did. One dear friend of mine almost lost his marriage because of sexual addiction. The stuff that came out was seriously embarrassing for him and could have easily ended his marriage. But I'll never forget when he said, "Bobby, I love my wife. With all my heart I want to stay with her, and she has every right to leave me. But even if she does, even though I'd be brokenhearted, I'm so glad I'm not alone in this anymore and that I'm not carrying around the terrible burden of a lie."

In every case people who open up about a deep, dark secret are incredibly glad to be alive and real again. There's no lie, nothing hidden. The process is always messy. But the response is always more gracious and supportive than you'd think, and everyone finds so much peace and joy when they are finally out with it. This is why criminals turn themselves in so often. That used to confuse me. Why would someone who got away with the crime and has continued to get away with it for years, suddenly turn up and turn himself in? Because the burden of hiding and of lying is never worth it.

I liken it to spring cleaning. We all clean our houses once or twice a week. We pick up the kids' toys, make the beds, and sort everything into the right places. Sometimes we do a deep clean with Windex and even get that nasty spot behind the toilet. But maybe every year or so, we do a full-blown spring cleaning. We pull the furniture away from the walls. Closets and drawers are purged of the random junk that's piled up over the year. Spring cleaning means everything is going to get even untidier before it gets truly clean. Spring cleaning makes a mess before it makes a clean house.

That's what true vulnerability looks like. Whether you're talking about your deepest fears and worries or saying no honestly or confessing something that's been lingering for a while, extreme vulnerability leads to extreme joy and ultimately extreme energy. You can't always make people happy, and you can't meet all the demands and pressures that are put on you. So reject those demands and pressures, and you'll take one step closer to a life full of emotional energy.

10

YOU DON'T HAVE TO WORRY

Jesus was relaxed.

—Dallas Willard

I am not the sort of person who likes to let go or give up control. When something bad happens, my natural inclination is to hustle my way through or manufacture a result different than the one prescribed for me. In some ways, this resolve and drive has led to success in my life, and I'm thankful for that. However, I'm learning very quickly that my greatest victories have not been the ones I've manufactured or hustled for; they are the ones that fell into my lap when I learned to let go. I am still learning to let go, and the more I learn that, the happier and more successful I am.

If you are human, you are likely going through something right now. It might be big, or it might be small, but my guess is you can probably tell me fairly quickly what it is you're going through. I want you to know, God is going to get you through whatever it is. It won't be the last time you deal with issues, and I know it isn't the first. Just know you and God will get through this. You can relax.

117

Worry

Life can be an anxious experience. The word *worry* is used often in the Bible. The Greek word for *worry* (sometimes translated as "anxiety") is *merimnao*, which literally means "to be pulled apart." Or maybe we'd say "pulled in a million directions." The Latin word means something like "to be suffocated." These words help us give voice to a plaguing feeling most of us have every day: the thought that we're pulled in a million directions, we are not the masters of our destinies, and so many outside forces are working to ruin, divert, or delay our calling. *When will I get a rest or catch a break?* we wonder.

Our society continues to reinforce our worry with hysterical dooms-day news stories—or even worse, show us we are not living the life we could if we only tried a little harder. It's no wonder even the most successful and healthiest people in the world can live every day believing "This won't last long" or "The end is nigh." Feeling relaxed, with a smile on one's face, can be interpreted as lazy. Or worse, something only stupid people do.

The truth is the smartest people in the world are those who have learned to be successful, to do well in life, but to also endure suffering with a relaxed constitution and even joy. These people are called *Christians*. Above all, hope in the midst of suffering stands as the great stalwart against the dread and worry that entangles so many secular people. Christians believe God is at work for their benefit and loves them. They don't need clarity, only knowledge. They need to know the Word of God.

This is yet another reason why the church, with all its warts and imperfections, stands as the greatest hope for creation. The world is so negative. It's negative about the future, about government, about every news story, and about you. The world subtly says you are simply not enough—not thin enough, smart enough, rich enough, or young enough. The church, on the other hand, is called to be a shining beacon of hope for the sick, the poor, and the elderly—the "least of these" (see Matt. 25). It says if you walk by faith you will have a bright future. It teaches its disciples to work and live from a positive place of vision and belief. Believing in destiny, heaven, the love of God, and the idea that heaven itself is breaking into Earth gives the true Christian the sometimes opaque yet hopeful vision for a way forward for everyone else. That's you. You are not a worrisome person. You know the character of God. You know he will get us through this. You are a hopeful visionary who can see a way forward.

The Fantasy (Relaxing)

Do you fantasize about a worry-free life? We all do, sometimes unconsciously. When things are really hard, we find ourselves daydreaming about being somewhere else without a care in the world. I always picture someplace tropical; I imagine myself lying out on a dock somewhere in the Caribbean. I've been there for a long time, maybe years, without a care in the world. The weather is great. The dock I'm lying on is wooden, and next to it is my little fishing boat. The wind wafts through the palm trees, and a vast emerald sea murmurs around me. I don't have a care in the world.

I asked Hannah if she ever did this, and the answer was a resounding yes. Only hers wasn't tropical, it was forested. She always pictures herself in a stone house with a thatched roof, moss on top, somewhere in England, like the Dover cliffs. There she goes on sunny, carefree, windy walks, as if she were Elizabeth Bennett in the *Pride and Prejudice* movie. She said this was likely her fantasy because growing up in Oklahoma she was often around forests and trees, exploring the wilderness.

It's funny, because both of our fantasies are connected to our childhood. I spent lots of time on my dad's little fishing boat, exploring little islands in Mexico or taking mini trips to Catalina Island. Hannah grew up in Native American country in Tahlequah, Oklahoma. For both of us, our unique fantasies oddly find us in a world similar to those we were in as children—the times when we had the fewest worries, no bills, no finals, no kids, and very little pressure.

The feeling we long for is not to be in a beautiful place, but rather to be in a state of mind that is relaxed, without a worry or care in the world. That's the real fantasy. The truth is if that can't exist now, it likely can't exist if we are jobless millionaires on a deserted island somewhere.

I remember years ago when Hannah and I were doing ministry and our lives were much less stressful and rigorous than they are now. I specifically remember we had saved up for a vacation to Hawaii for our anniversary. I couldn't wait to go.

When we arrived, we instantly switched to "go mode." We got the rental car (which took forever—maybe two hours), then had to load up on groceries since we were staying at a friend's apartment. When we got there, we had to go through a number of loopholes to get our keys. I was feeling angry at this point. I wanted to hurry up and relax.

When we opened the wide glass doors overlooking the water, with warm breezes and the sound of ocean waves filling the room, I knew we had arrived in paradise.

Oddly, it took several days for me to get out of "go mode." I found myself constantly bored or antsy. I had been in high-adrenaline mode for so long I really didn't know what to do with myself when I had little or nothing to occupy my time. Half the trip was gone before I realized I hadn't relaxed yet. Now I started worrying about how few days I had left to reach my goal of total relaxation. Though the trip was great all in all, it was a wake-up call for me that being relaxed relies on training and a constant state of mind. Since that trip I have received the knowledge to realize most of the time we can be relaxed. We don't need Hawaii.

That is the great hope. The fantasy is attainable today! Unless you are currently going through some major trauma or have a brain-chemistry issue, you can live in a relaxed state of mind while being successful professionally or as a parent or both. In fact, being relaxed rather than constantly worrying will make you a better professional, leader, parent, and friend because you will empower others instead of controlling them.

Jesus painted the picture of a worry-free life:

Therefore I tell you, do not worry about your life, what you will eat or drink; or about your body, what you will wear. Is not life more than food, and the body more than clothes? Look at the birds of the air; they do not sow or reap or store away in barns, and yet your heavenly Father feeds them. Are you not much more valuable than they? Can any one of you by worrying add a single hour to your life?

And why do you worry about clothes? See how the flowers of the field grow. They do not labor or spin. Yet I tell you that not even Solomon in all his splendor was dressed like one of these. If that is how God clothes the grass of the field, which is here today and tomorrow is thrown into the fire, will he not much more clothe you—you of little faith? (Matt. 6:25–30)

It is interesting to watch birds at play on a sunny day. Sometimes when I go running through the hills near my home and the weather is beautiful, I'll see these terrible clouds of flies. And then little sparrows will start swooping through, eating them up as though it's a game. It's fun to watch, not only because I hate bugs but because the birds look almost like children at play. They are relaxed, just as Jesus said. The Lord does care for them. Looking at them brings to my own mind a better day when things weren't so complicated.

As I keep running, I look and see the lilies of the field as well, so colorful in spring after a good rain. It's funny to think of a flower as being relaxed, but they are and are being cared for in every moment by the Father. Jesus told us the greatest king in history wasn't dressed up as beautifully as these. How much more will God make sure we have the clothing we need?

As mentioned in chapter 6 of this book, Jesus finished by saying in Matthew 6, "Don't worry about these things, because they are the empty things pagans run after. And by the way, your Father knows you need them. So seek after his kingdom and his righteousness, and God will make sure you have all the earthly stuff you require." What a promise. The "seek ye first," passage here is one of the most important in the Bible because it tells us where to focus our energy.

Your Soul Is Like a Battery

Your mental focus is a bit like bandwidth: you only have so much. As we build up lots of little things to concern ourselves with, we quickly find our available space is full.

The soul is a bit like a laptop battery. When a battery is new and fresh, it seems to last forever. You plug it in at night, but you almost don't have to. You still have 60 percent. As the computer gets older, though, there are more programs running, most of them hidden. There's malware, spyware, and antivirus programs using energy to protect the computer. Now, after a couple of years, even when no programs are open, the battery depletes very quickly.

Finally, some tech-savvy friend of yours goes through the computer and shuts down all those hidden programs that eat up the life of your battery. And *bam*, you get your old computer back.

The soul is a bit like that. There are so many things going on unconsciously that eat away at your energy. Unexpressed stresses and disappointments, lack of rest or recreation, hidden fears and anxieties are all just a few of the things that gnaw away at our spiritual stamina. As we mentioned earlier, the greatest drain we have is the lack of bonding deeply with others. It's unlikely that long-lasting passion and desire for anything will exist with all these other things going on behind the scenes.

In their book *Willpower*, Roy Baumeister and John Tierney prove scientifically that every person has a certain amount of willpower. They paint the picture of something like a gas tank. As the day goes on little things make withdrawals from your willpower. Making decisions, working, and trying to lose weight are a few examples. But nothing drains you like chronic worry. Having too much on your mind quickly eats away at your willpower, the stuff you need to push through difficult circumstances.[1] That's ironic, right? By worrying about what might happen in the future, you're actually draining your mind of the energy you would need to emotionally get through that event.

You only have so much you can think about. As you think about all the bad things that might happen, you will quickly lose the power to dream about all the wonderful things that could happen. Worrying about what we'll eat or wear can quickly divert us from seeing the big calling God has for us.

Worry Distracts

You can't do everything, and you must know your limitations. Worry keeps us from focusing on the one or two projects in life that really give us passion and joy. Once I was playing chess with a college kid. We were having a great conversation about life and career. After a long silence with both of us enthralled in the game, he leaned back and asked, "How can I become a millionaire?" It was a strange question, as I myself am not a millionaire, but I did have an answer.

I asked, "Are you a moral man?"

"To the best of my ability," he replied.

Then, without even thinking about it, I said, "Be the best at something."

I've seen it over and over with the world's richest people. Most of them never really set out to be wealthy. Rather they set out to make or do something excellent. For many of them, money is more a way to keep score. It's a game. If the stories about Facebook founder Mark Zuckerberg are true, he was offered millions of dollars multiple times to sell Facebook before it became clear whether or not it would even be a success. He didn't care and didn't sell because he had a big vision to build a worldwide social network. People who become the best at anything, even hobbies like chess, usually do very well financially.

Conversely, I had lots of friends in business school that set out to be millionaires. They had pictures of luxury cars in their dorm rooms and talked constantly about how to make millions. I've only kept up with a couple of them, but none of them are millionaires. Their dream was not to make something great or to be someone great. It was just lust.

Not long ago, another acquaintance of mine set out to build a business with the original intent to "sell it for millions." He never made anything special and sold his business for less than he put into it.

I don't say this to gloat. He and others at least started something. But I've learned by watching: those who build a great dream, or those who invest in themselves, tend to have the money thing well taken care of as a byproduct.

You can't shoot to be something as abstract as a millionaire and live with focus. You can't have your mind pulled apart in a million directions and expect to succeed in any aspect of your life, whether it is business, family, or faith. Worry keeps us from focusing.

You Can Let Go

All earthly power is temporary. It's an illusion to think the power we've been given will last forever. In the end we will have to let go. Many people in society talk about "letting it go." (Having a young daughter, the *Frozen* song comes to mind.) The Christian life is a journey of letting go, because doing so is how you trust. Letting go doesn't mean it's not important; it means you're placing your power and control in the very strong arms of God.

The art of letting go is rooted in a dynamic relationship with God. When you know him personally and know his character, letting go becomes the only natural thing to do. I am not strong enough to handle sickness, depression, worry, and especially my own death. Neither are you. And yet every time you give something over to God, you receive something better by faith. In the Christian tradition this is called the Paschal Mystery. Like a phoenix, by faith all our ashes and loss will be raised into new life. Every exit becomes an entrance. Every death is the birth of something new. In this way, as we let

> The Christian life is a journey of letting go, because doing so is how you trust.

go of really important things, we can trust that in the end only good can come from it. Even when we breathe our last, we receive the goodness of heaven and eternal life. It's good to get in the habit of letting go before the ultimate letting go of your heartbeat.

Nouwen and the Circus

Ronald Rolheiser called Henri Nouwen "this generation's Kierkegaard." That's very much what he was. He dealt with the complexities, tragedies, and beauties of existence and offered the reader a sort of written empathy. By reading Nouwen and glimpsing his vulnerability and heart, you see a lonely man yearning to live every moment in the love of God. I never met Nouwen before he died in 1996, but I feel as though I've come to know him through his writings and his many friends. He seems to me someone who desperately wanted to live out what he was writing about but often struggled to do so. He seemed a restless man, always on the go. Yet it's from many of his stories and engagements with the world and with people that some of his best writing comes.

One of my favorites is how he got wrapped up traveling with a circus trapeze troupe. A couple of his friends invited his dad and him to go see The Flying Rodleighs at the German circus Simoneit-Barum. He loved it so much that he went back again the next day and, after the show, introduced himself to the trapeze group. Of course, they hit it off with Nouwen. They invited him to come to their practices (which he did), gave him free tickets to shows, and eventually they became friends. Over dinner one night they said, "You should travel with us for a while!"

He did.

On tour he had a long talk with the flyer—the star acrobat who flips and flies through the air—of the troupe. From this conversation comes one of my favorite metaphors of the spiritual life. In Nouwen's words:

125

One day, I was sitting with Rodleigh, the leader of the troupe, in his caravan, talking about flying. He said, "As a flyer, I must have complete trust in my catcher. The public might think that I am the great star of the trapeze, but the real star is Joe, my catcher. He has to be there for me with split-second precision and grab me out of the air as I come to him in the long jump."

"How does it work?" I asked.

"The secret," Rodleigh said, "is that the flyer does nothing and the catcher does everything. When I fly to Joe, I have simply to stretch out my arms and hands and wait for him to catch me and pull me safely over the apron behind the catchbar."

"You do nothing!" I said, surprised.

"Nothing," Rodleigh repeated. "The worst thing the flyer can do is to try to catch the catcher. I am not supposed to catch Joe. It's Joe's task to catch me. If I grabbed Joe's wrists, I might break them, or he might break mine, and that would be the end for both of us. A flyer must fly, and a catcher must catch, and the flyer must trust, with outstretched arms, that his catcher will be there for him."[2]

This is the way to live life. As we soar from one thing to the next, we must do so with a spirit of trust. Freaking out only makes things worse, and worrying takes away the joy of the flight. Simply move with the wind of the Spirit of God and reach out your arms. Don't try and catch him. He'll catch you. Today you can relax and smile.

There is so much in life you can't control. Worrying about something that might happen, that you couldn't control anyway, is a total waste of energy. Better for you to have lots of energy when something bad happens. Then you will have your wits about you, as well as your strength, and you'll endure the challenge better. In short, people who don't constantly worry are better prepared for the challenges of life than those who do worry and see them coming.

Relaxing and not worrying doesn't mean you give up. It simply means you don't waste your time on something that *might* happen. It means you live every day with joy, expectancy, and even hard work. You can be very responsible without worrying. You can work hard while relaxed. In fact, this is the ideal.

I once read a story of a man whose life was totally changed when he heard the words, "Life is not happening to you. It is happening for you."[3] This simple shift in the way you view your circumstance can change everything about the way you experience adversity. The idea that life is happening for you allows you to hold the future loosely.

You can believe this because God is the God of life and he's for you. Even when you are lost in sin, he is for you, leading you in the direction of becoming a better you. The perspective of "Life is not happening to me, but for me," gives you a grateful and positive outlook on life—the kind that says, "I know God is good and he will sort this out, so I don't have to worry about it." Faith is not about leaps, but rather about continually trusting God in the midst of loss, challenge, confusion, and doubt. Faith says, "I'm going to do my best and forget the rest. God has this under control, and I can let go."

Training Ourselves to Relax

The best way to relax is to train our minds in that direction. Training means continually moving something in a direction it wouldn't naturally go. Dogs are not naturally house-trained, but many have successfully mastered that task. I trained my bougainvillea to grow in an arch over the gate to our backyard. It didn't want to grow that way; it wanted to grow upward in the direction of the sun.

It's not natural for your mind to be relaxed and positive. It's natural to be negative. Being hopeful and trusting is hard work. Being cynical and worried is what everyone else does.

Much of the training to combat that involves taking every thought captive. When you worry about something, give it to God in prayer. Realign your thoughts with Scripture and with the knowledge of God's goodness. It's not really training to just shove it down and ignore it. Rather, give it to God through your rested times of prayer and meditation. Then act on faith rather than fear. Do what you would do if you weren't worried. At first many of these things will feel unnatural, but over time they will become life-giving habits and you'll find being less anxious will come more naturally.

The second way to train your mind out of worry is to walk with a soul-friend. I don't mean to belabor this point, but when you feel anxious about something you need to experience empathy. In a way, by just saying it aloud to a loving empathetic person, you deflate much of what made you nervous in the first place. You'll find that getting it off your chest, even if it's silly, will cause you to have more energy and promote a more hopeful view of things. Soul-friends, if they're doing a good job, are going to really do their best to feel what you're feeling, validate it, and probably give you a big bear hug. Sometimes that's all you need.

The main thing is not to be okay with dwelling on your fears. Make it a priority that you "refuse to live like this." Notice the pain that worry is causing and decide from the outset that you will take it captive and not fixate on it. You will act in the opposite direction of worry and ask for help. The less willing you are to ask for help, the more likely you need it.

Clear Eyes

Letting go of worry and abandoning outcomes gives us relaxed eyes to see brightly. As business strategist and author Dave Martin said, "Tired eyes can't see a bright future." Worry is the result of looking into the future and trying to predict something bad that might happen in the hopes of having some impact on the outcome. But this kind of vision only leaves us with tired eyes. It's contrary to the kind of possibility thinking that leads to radical breakthroughs in your life and to the great relationships that will make all the difference.

When you relax your vision of the future, you see all the good things that could happen. You fall in love with possibility. That breeds hope, endurance, and victory. As you achieve one win after another, you build clear eyes that can see a hopeful way forward. That kind of vision only comes when you let go of trying to control the future.

It's like looking at a stereogram. You might remember those strange computer-animated 3-D images from the nineties. As you look at a stereogram you naturally see a two-dimensional image. It's nothing particularly interesting—usually a bunch of random shapes and colors like a kaleidoscope. But if you can relax your eyes and look through the two-dimensional image, you will see a three-dimensional image hidden within the stereogram. It's like a puzzle.

For some people it is impossible to see this image. Many refuse to believe there's actually something there. But when you see it, it's very cool, and you also feel quite proud of yourself.

Dr. Doug DiSiena explained that looking at a stereogram is actually good for you. In order to do it, your mind has to relax as if you were meditating. By being more relaxed you're able to see beyond the two-dimensional illusion to the real picture beyond. Trying harder can stress you out and make the 3-D image more elusive. He said:

> That "efforting" will only cause more eye strain and you will never see the hidden image. Paradoxically, as you relax and thus your eyes see through the image, the 3-D image appears. By relaxing, we calm stress hormones, and we push cerebral activity to the neocortex. That's where higher functions of the brain occur like creativity, reasoning, and language.[4]

Seeing by faith is the same way. You must let everything go to God, and only then will he show you. You must stop fixating on the two-dimensionality of your circumstances. You must relax your eyes and see farther and deeper. But you can only do that when you trust.

Worrying is all about control. Faith is all about empowering. When we are worried, we are essentially trying to control outcomes and people.

This leads to drained energy and an unsuccessful life. When we live by faith, we are okay with people making mistakes. We don't have to fix everything or everyone. We are still responsible, but we live within our limitations. It is here we move from controlling people and outcomes to empowering people and possibilities. When you become an empowering versus a controlling person, you are a better leader, a better parent, and a better friend. You will quite naturally attract good things in your life, and you'll have more energy than you would if you spent your time trying to keep the plates spinning.

The best feeling in the world is not worrying about the future. It matters, but we don't allow it to ruin the present. At the start of the *Lord of the Rings* trilogy, the hobbits have already gone through hell and still have more hell ahead of them. But they get a break in the city of Rivendell. Something about the place allows them to refresh their hearts and minds. Tolkien wrote, "The future, good or ill, was not forgotten, but ceased to have any power over the present. Health and hope grew strong in them, and they were content with each good day as it came, taking pleasure in every meal, and in every word and song."[5]

I wish this over you. Wherever God is, heaven is. If he is with you, heaven is with you and you deserve a reprieve from the suffering of life. Today you get to relax, enjoy every friend and every meal, and know that you do enough and you are enough. You are loved by God.

11

YOU DON'T HAVE TO WORRY—
HOW TO VIEW STRESS

What lies behind us and what lies before us are
tiny matters compared to what lies within us.
—Unknown

God doesn't want you to worry, because that robs you of life and energy. That doesn't mean he will give you a stress-free life. Stress can be good!

As a broad stroke, worry is bad for you. However, although it might feel strange to read this, stress, if handled the right way, is good for you. It makes you stronger, pushes you to new places, and keeps you from becoming complacent in your life. It's very likely that when you think of times of adversity, they were also the times you grew the most. Stress is the pressure that makes us better—as long as we have the tools to understand its place in our life. It will be good for your soul and your body as long as you don't hold it too long, and as long as you don't internalize it. (More on this later—it's the key.)

No one has just one calling. God asks us to do lots of things in life, not just one big task. Much of life is an experience of peaks and valleys, highs and lows, in achievement. Through it all, the stresses we face prepare us for our next calling. Seminary was very stressful for me. I had to learn two ancient languages and spar intellectually with people who were smarter than me. I had to read tons of books and pulled many all-nighters. At no point did I think school was there only to stress me out. I believed through the whole process the stress was good for me—the training I needed for my next calling. I thought it was a privilege to be there, even though at times I hated it.

Though you may not feel it, it's likely that many of the things you're going through are actually a part of some preparation for the next big thing you'll do for God.

Paul gives us a great metaphor for the kind of stress that brings out the best in us. He said:

> We have this treasure in jars of clay to show that this all-surpassing power is from God and not from us. We are hard pressed on every side, but not crushed; perplexed, but not in despair; persecuted, but not abandoned; struck down, but not destroyed. We always carry around in our body the death of Jesus, so that the life of Jesus may also be revealed in our body. (2 Cor. 4:7–10)

The metaphor of the clay jar as a representation of the human body was common in ancient Judaism. In the Genesis account God fashioned the bodies of Adam and Eve from the dust of the earth. In Paul's time clay jars were everyday kinds of things, similar to plastic or glass in our day. Even today, if you go to an archaeological dig somewhere in Israel or Turkey, you'll see broken bits of ancient pottery all over. It's quite fascinating, actually. There are little two-thousand-year-old bits of clay from a people long gone, all of them in jagged shapes just laying around. Most places you can pick one up and put it in your pocket. No one cares because pottery in the ancient world was on par with something like Tupperware today. It was everywhere, and it was cheap.

Paul was saying we are a bit like that, like everyday clay jars that everyone thinks are normal and mundane. Little do they know there's this amazing treasure hidden within our body—both the death and life of Jesus, which gives us a sort of resurrection power in our everyday living. It's as though life itself tries to crush us, confuse us, and break us, but we endure to victory because of what is within.

This is a great passage in a discussion about stress because stress is pressure from our environment. This is what Paul experienced all the time. The name *Paul* means "short," and it was likely he was a little guy, maybe also a bit socially awkward. It seems like he didn't have loads of friends and yet still had to lead and make big decisions about the church. His Jewish peers, many of whom didn't think the gospel was for Gentiles, constantly pressed him. He was dealing with a nascent church divided on theology, practice, culture, and a million other things.

> It's as though life itself tries to crush us, confuse us, and break us, but we endure to victory because of what is within.

He was also likely perplexed, as God had him going from this town to that with seemingly no rhyme or reason. He started traveling to India and God said, "No, not that way." He was shipwrecked. He had people sabotaging his work. Once, in Lystra, a mob tried to stone him to death. They didn't kill him, though, and after regaining consciousness, he just got up and started preaching again. He was a honey badger.

The takeaway is that Paul was telling his audience, many of whom were facing similar trials, "Don't worry. You won't break or be destroyed. The treasure within you, the life and death of Christ, will get you through this. It will make you stronger and show God's glory to the world." That message is the same for us today. Life will hit you, press you, confuse you, but won't break you. Those experiences will train you and make you stronger.

Distress Versus Eustress

The way we view and experience stress makes all the difference. When we deal with stress in a good way, it becomes eustress. In Greek the word *eu* means "it's good." The word *eustress* means that the stress you're experiencing is good for you and is healthy for normal development. However, when stress is internalized—meaning it's still there but it's unconscious—or when we hold stress too long, it becomes distress. It eats away at our body and soul.

As our society has become more affluent, it has also become more comfortable and safe. Comfort and safety are great, but like food or anything else in life, we can have too much of it. When we've been in a comfortable place for too long, we can actually become trapped, gripped by a fear of pain or failure. It's times like these that we need new challenges in our lives to knock us out of the rut.

In a recent study, *Harvard Business Review* found that the most important thing in handling stress is to simply have a positive view of stress in general. If you listen to most of society, everyone only talks about the negatives of stress. But this is a mistake because it causes people to see stress as a curse to be avoided rather than the very thing that causes us to grow and develop into better versions of ourselves. This Harvard study showed, however, that people under stress had greater mental toughness, deeper relationships, heightened awareness, new perspectives, a sense of mastery, a greater appreciation for life, a heightened sense of meaning, and strengthened priorities.

Stress isn't bad for you. It's life's pressure that makes you stronger. Stress trains your character as the gym trains the body. Bodybuilders and athletes in the gym are constantly adding more weights because they want to get stronger. The pressure the weights put on their body makes them much stronger than the rest of us. They know if they put on too much weight, they can get injured, or if they put on too little weight, they won't make any progress at all. Stress is the gym of life. Too much of it for too long will injure your soul, but not enough will make you weak and afraid.

I love the way the American Hasidic rabbi and psychologist Abraham Twerski put it. He told a story of sitting in a waiting room. From his chair he looked down and saw an article, *How Does a Lobster Grow?* Bored and a touch curious, he began to read.

Lobsters grow but their shells don't, he learned. The shell works as a protective shield from predatory fish but also can be the thing that makes them uncomfortable. As time goes by, the pressure from the shell becomes so uncomfortable that they go under a rock, shed the shell, and a new one grows on their soft little bodies. Then, as they continue to grow, they return to the rock, shed the shell, and get an even bigger one.

Twerski's point is, "The stimulus for growth is that the lobster feels uncomfortable." The pressure from the shell is the very thing that forces the lobster to go and get a new one. The lobster doesn't hang onto its old shell, lamenting what a fine thing it was. Because of pressure and discomfort, it embraces the new shell and carries on bigger and better than it was before.[1]

Being married and having children will make you mature at an exponential rate. Married men and women receive instant pressure and accountability to be better. Having children does it even more. Parents don't get to sleep much when a baby is born. Then, when the babies become little kids, they have to go to tons of events. And teenagers are a constant source of hormonal neurosis. These things only make the parents tougher. This is only conjecture, but I've noticed parents tend to be way less uptight about things like politics, religion, or holding grudges. After all, they've got kids to worry about.

Stress Makes You Strong

God will use failures, disappointments, and setbacks if you let him. It's all practice for what he has next for you.

To begin, when I was nineteen, I was asked to go to Germany and cover the World's Fair. I was just a kid, a business major with zero experience in media or television. For whatever reason, though, I was offered an internship (meaning they didn't pay me anything) to be the host of a Canadian television program. For me, a free six-month stay in Germany sounded like a dream, so of course I said yes.

I was terrible in front of the camera. There's something about cameras that makes talking like a normal human being feel impossible. I had so many failed takes that our camera crew would take lunch breaks in the middle of shooting a basic segment. I felt so bad. I was ruining everyone's day. I'm pretty sure no one wanted to shoot with me.

Toward the end of the six-month internship, I was getting better. But as we were now drawing to the end of the fair, it felt too late, and I wondered if much of the content I made was unusable. I had gone to Germany hoping to make a difference, but I went home wondering if I was a disappointment to the team.

Years later I was invited by a major production company in LA to be a judge on a reality-TV program called *The Messengers*. I was thrilled by the opportunity. I was just a seminary student but now felt pretty good in front of a camera. The show was about people from different parts of America with a wide range of religious views, including atheism, who would give speeches on various social, political, and spiritual issues. My job was to be the religion "expert" and judge the content of the speeches. Then the live audience would decide each week which candidate had to go. The ultimate goal was to whittle down one speaker each week until we arrived at the final person, who would be deemed America's Next Inspirational Speaker.

The whole thing was picked up by TLC, who in turn made *The Messengers* their flagship program for the coming TV year. This time I got paid—a lot—and they were already talking about doing a season two. I thought I had won the lottery, that this was going to be my gig. Would I be famous? As a young twenty-seven-year-old, I had very high hopes.

How did it do? Well, let me ask you, have you ever heard of or seen *The Messengers*? It was a flop. The ratings weren't terrible, but they weren't great either. Just as they were debating a season two, the great recession of 2008 happened, and TLC pulled back. My dream was crushed.

Both experiences were incredibly stressful and included tons of work. To make it worse, both experiences were more or less failures, to the point of being embarrassing. I had no idea that ten years later I would be preaching to millions on television. Preaching on TV was never a dream of mine. In general, I didn't have a stellar opinion of so-called televangelists, and I hadn't started *Hour of Power*. But as soon as I stepped into the role, it felt natural, like my whole life had trained me for this. The stress, failure, and loss of my past were just the things I needed to carry this calling in this season of my life.

Stress is good for you as long as you have the right tools to make it eustress instead of distress. The pressures you feel in your job, in parenting, or even in your relationships are maturing you and usually have a hand in your next big calling. The key is employing both methods— don't internalize stress and don't hold it too long without taking a break.

Don't Internalize Stress

The stress and trauma we experience in life leaves little wounds on the soul. It's almost like every time you go through something stressful, it can be akin to something as little as the sore muscles you feel the day after a new workout or as big as the bumps and bruises you get after tripping and falling. Sometimes it can be full-on blunt-force trauma, like when a bone breaks or you get a deep cut. The worse the stressful experience is, the more you need help from others. Just as you wouldn't try to give yourself stitches, you shouldn't try and navigate a traumatic experience alone. And furthermore, there's no need to navigate something like a stressful day of work or parenting alone. You need friends to help you.

The dangers of the wound and process of healing are also very similar to normative medical wounds you'd get on your body. Say you were in a terrible car accident. Would you rather have a bunch of nasty cuts on your chest, arms, and legs, or would you rather have broken bones and internalized bleeding? (I know you want to say neither, but humor me for the argument.) Given this terrible choice, everyone would choose the visible cuts. They are visible and therefore treatable. They may not look pretty, but they likely won't kill you, and the recovery will be quick.

Internal wounds, however, are extremely dangerous. The victim may look okay on the outside, with maybe a couple of bruises, but internal bleeding or ruptured organs might possibly kill the patient or cause long-term damage to the body.

In the same way, you usually have a choice on what to do with your stress. It's a wound. It happened. Still, you get to choose whether it's an internal wound (one that will threaten the life of your soul) or an external wound (one that will likely not cause long-term harm). The way you choose to make it external is by talking at length about it with an empathetic friend. As you talk about your stressful day—how someone disrespected you, how you felt like a wallflower, how you feel you aren't where you want to be, or how your day was super demanding—you'll move that stress wound from the inside to the outside. Though these examples may seem benign, ignoring the little triggers as "not worth talking about" can actually lead to shame and internalizing emotions. It's in that space that your friends can, like a medic, treat you and help you recover quickly and be much stronger.

I can't emphasize this enough: I can tell you from personal experience that internalizing stress can lead to real physical health problems and pathology. For me, I experienced emotional numbness for years. I'll never go back to that place.

Stress doesn't make you tough by internalizing it. It actually makes you weak. Talking with close friends or a spouse about the pressures in life cause the stress to become the kind of healthy adversity that grows us. It's easy to say, "Oh, it's no big deal. I'm not going to bother them with such a little thing." But even the little things can cause great harm to your soul the same way the smallest object or fracture in your body can get infected and cause considerable damage. Besides, most friends don't consider it weakness or a burden. They consider it an honor, and they will trust you and like you more.

I don't consider someone a dear friend unless I've emotionally bled in front of him or her. If they've never heard me share a tough experience or seen me cry or get angry, then we likely haven't connected in a deep enough way to be great friends. It's not like we sit around all day talking about our feelings, but I always know that over a meal or a cup of coffee, I'm going to have a few minutes to say what's weighing on my mind. I also know I'm likely to get a "non-fix-you" quiet and loving presence and probably a hug. That's good stuff.

You may have guessed the one I connect the most deeply with in this way is my wife, Hannah. Every night we set aside some time to pray and talk about the day. One of the questions we ask each other that forces us to talk about stress is: "What was your high and low today?" (I got this question from Mentor Bill and I can't tell you how helpful it has been.) By being asked this question I am forced to look back on how I experienced my day emotionally. So many times my first thought has been, "I didn't have any lows today" only to realize something rough happened, but I'd already internalized it. If I hadn't thought through it and received empathy from Hannah, that memory would have gone to an unconscious place and caused me increased anxiety and distress. It would have drained my battery for days, and I would have found myself wondering why I felt tired.

If you don't have a friendship like this, I can't emphasize enough how important it is to get one. The ancient Christian writers referred to this as a *soul-friend*. Having a soul-friend may be the most important thing to help you grow in energy, joy, and holiness. If you're married, your spouse is the obvious choice, although I also think it's best to have multiple soul-friendships. I would try to find a friend at church, join a small group, or simply show parts of this chapter to a friend you already have but want to go deeper with. Maybe consider making it a point to get on the phone every night, or at least once a week, and ask, "What was your high and low?" Any work in this regard will reap so much benefit in your life, it's difficult to overstate.

Put the Cup Down

Rest is a scriptural mandate. It's also one of the biblical commands most ignored by American Christians. Many Jewish rabbis spent time talking about how one of the great benefits of the biblical creation story is to show us even God rested. Non-rest is akin to saying, "I can do it better than God."

I don't say that to make you feel guilty, but just the opposite. Many of us are so fixated on our identity, success, and work that we never rest. We feel guilty if we relax and watch a movie, or if we take the day off from work to have fun. We feel guilty if we take a nap. Jesus took naps. If you ever feel guilty taking naps, just say to yourself, "I'm being Christlike."

Enduring stress for long periods of time is not good for you. Just like any other form of exercise, overdoing it can cause injury and make you less productive over the long run. Staying at a high point of pressure is really hard on your mind and body, so don't do it. You need a break.

I read a story once of a psychologist who was trying to explain this principle to her audience. She held up a glass that was half full of water. Naturally, everyone thought she was going to give another lecture on having a positive outlook or something. Instead, she asked, "How heavy is this glass of water?"

Surprised by the question, people started guessing. "A hundred grams? Five hundred grams?"

She told them, "Actually, the weight doesn't matter except to know it's not that heavy. Would it be difficult for me to hold this glass of water for two minutes? Not really. But what if I held it all day," she asked. "After a while my arm would start trembling, the glass would get heavier and heavier, then my arm would cramp up, and eventually it would be totally paralyzed." She said, "The point is not how heavy it is, but rather that no matter how strong I am, I cannot hold it forever. I must put the glass down."

Stress is the same way. What at first seems light becomes a terrible burden if we hold it too long. You must make time to relax and not just go do something else stressful. Relax, rest, and have fun, or even the smallest things will wear you out.

12

YOU DON'T HAVE TO HURRY

I have no time to be in a hurry.
—Henry David Thoreau

You don't have to hurry. You can have long empty spaces between the events of your life, and you can go somewhere slowly. You can cultivate good time management and arrive early rather than race up at the last minute. You can live at a walking pace. Life is too good to be hurried.

In *Christianity Today* John Ortberg wrote about how he first began a job in Chicago at one of the largest churches in America. It was at a time in his life when he had lots of personal needs at home, including taking the kids to piano practice and sports, while at the same time many needs at his new job. He was in a place where he was happy but could tell things were not right in his inner life. He needed council on the state of his spirit and called his old friend and mentor Dallas Willard. After explaining how he felt stressed and overwhelmed and struggled daily wondering if he was pleasing God, he asked Dallas over the phone, "What do I need to do to be spiritually healthy?" Here's his account:

[Dallas gave a] long pause . . . "You must ruthlessly eliminate hurry from your life," he said at last . . .

Another long pause.

"Okay, I've written that one down," I told him a little impatiently. "That's a good one. Now what else is there?" I had a lot of things to do and this was a long-distance call so I was anxious to cram as many units of spiritual wisdom into the least amount of time possible.

Another long pause.

"There is nothing else," he said. "You must ruthlessly eliminate hurry from your life."[1]

Dallas was known to say this to many people. It was in fact one of his more famous sayings. He felt strongly that life couldn't be good in a hurry and people couldn't be good in a hurry. He said, "You can't be compassionate and in a hurry." He was right.

If you look at the Father's world, very little of it develops or grows quickly. In fact, the better it is, the slower it develops. Plants can take years to bear fruit, sequoias take centuries to reach their height, and mountains take millennia to rise from the earth. In the same way, disciples develop at the Father's pace. They are not built like a machine, but rather grown like a plant. The soul can't be nourished or joyful when hurried.

Is There Ever Enough Time?

It's easy to feel like a slave to time. We say things like, "There's not enough time in the day," and "Life is short." These clichés are underpinned by a feeling we all have: we just don't have enough time to be who we want to be. If only we had longer lives or longer days, we could make more time to do what we really love.

It's not likely. What's more probable is that extra time would be filled with extra responsibility and calendar clutter. There are two types of people in the world: those who master time and those who are mastered by it.

Our contempt for time is most reflected in the emotions we feel when we think of calendars, daily schedules, and especially clocks. What feelings come to mind when you think of clocks? Usually it's not a good feeling. Clocks remind us of deadlines, of being forced to wake up even though we're still tired, or of death itself. The Grim Reaper, for example, is often portrayed as the dark lich holding a scythe in one hand and an hourglass in the other. Father Time and the Grim Reaper seem to be buddies in this way—perhaps two faces of the same person.

Clocks shouldn't create such a daunting feeling in us. The fear of time shouldn't grip our lives in this way.

There's a historic irony in the original intent of the invention of the mechanical clock. Though there were many kinds of clocks before the medieval age, including contraptions such as water clocks and sundials, few were very efficient and rarely put to use. Later, in the eleventh and twelfth centuries, Benedictine monks invented the mechanical clock to help them keep track of their strict times for prayer. In fact, the word we use in English for clock is derived from the French word for *bell*. They invented the clock as a device that would chime bells every time they were supposed to pray. In other words, the original intent of the invention of the mechanical clock was to keep the brothers accountable to stop working and enter the chapel for rest and prayer. The clock was invented to get us to stop working.

Quite the opposite effect took place as the law of unintended consequences worked its way into fourteenth-century Europe. It was then that most Europeans started using the clock to sync up life, not for prayer but for work. Crystal-clear numbers were ascribed to time, and the idea of minutes and hours were gathered, traded, and viewed as a scarce commodity. Historian and philosopher Lewis Mumford wrote, "The mechanical clock made possible the idea of regular production, regular working hours and a standardized process." With the clock came the birth of industry. Time is money, you know. Mumford also said, "With the advent of the clock we moved from being time keepers, to time savers, to time servers."[2]

That is the state we find ourselves in: slaves to time. This looming fear of the clock is what initially trains us to live in a perpetual state of hurry. Habit is what keeps us there.

Clocks continue to get uglier. They've become less ornate, more plastic, and always more digital. Perhaps this change from beautiful to ugly is a reflection of the soul of our society and its slavery to and hatred for the measurement of time. America is the last holdout from switching to the even uglier military form of international time keeping. I pray I never have to say to my wife, "Sugar, it's twenty-three hundred hours. Time for bed."

Even the sweetest sounds we can pick as alarms on our phones eventually become incredibly annoying anytime we hear them. I remember when I once heard someone's phone ring with the same chime I use for my alarm clock in the morning. They seemed to take forever to answer it as each ring ground away at my ears. My brother used to have an alarm clock that sounded like fishing reel going off. At first we both loved it, but eventually this sound became so annoying to him I could chase him around the house with the little clock.

Time is a burden to us all. Hurry exacerbates it. What if, for one week, you made a decision to live at a restful pace—to begin, end, and go through every day unhurried?

Living Unhurried

A few years ago I did exactly that. It was in preparation for a sermon on living unhurried. I felt I needed to practice this if I wanted to preach it with any honesty. So I made a decision to ruthlessly eliminate hurry from my life for one week. I drove the speed limit every day. At restaurants I ordered slowly, paid slowly (tipped well), and ate every meal with gaps in between bites. I walked everywhere slowly and planned to get everywhere early so I wouldn't feel like I was delaying anyone. Anytime someone apologized for "taking too long" to do something, I would always say, "I'm not in a hurry," and smile. The smile was real.

The big takeaway is that I felt more pressure than I thought I would to return to my hurrying pace. I constantly felt like I was a bother or in someone's way. When I drove the speed limit in the right lane (where slowpokes are supposed to be), people would constantly ride up and speed around. I always enjoyed how, when driving on side streets, someone would go flying by only to halt abruptly at a stoplight. It would often turn green before I had to stop, which in turn had me zooming past them—at a relaxed speed of course.

Starbucks was the worst. I pay cash for everything, and as I got the change for my coffee, I would instantly feel shoved metaphorically by both the barista and the person behind me in line. As I put my change in my wallet (we're talking about three to four seconds), the barista was already looking at the guy behind me asking what she could get him, and he was nudging boldly into what I thought was my personal space. I really had to fight the temptation to say sorry for being in the way while shuffling to put my money away and holding my coffee somewhere else.

From restaurant servers to baristas to drivers to coworkers, I constantly felt disrespected, made to feel bothersome in a way I previously never had. This is because I had fallen out of sync with the hurried rhythms of society and into the easy rhythms of grace. I truly was in everyone's way. (I still am.) But the net result was I accomplished way more than when I was hurried. I was more productive, more energized, and a lot nicer to my wife and kids. I've done my best to stay with this habit, and it has changed my life. Hurrying doesn't make you faster. It makes you clumsy.

I realize being hurried is the new normal. I used to think elderly people were slow, but now I wonder if they just never got on board the hurry train of post-modernity. Maybe they're from a different era where it was okay to read the paper and have a cup of coffee for an hour.

We eat quickly in our cars. We give ourselves about two minutes less than we need to arrive on time, causing us to hurry to our next event. We freak out if a web page takes more than a second or two to load. And, unfortunately, we pray in a hurry. Prayer—that sacred moment where the soul communes with the God of the universe—has often devolved into a quick laundry list of needs lobbed up to heaven. There's little time for silence, discernment, and meditation. It's all about results.

Slowing Down Your Experience of Life

At the same time, there's a pesky feeling that life is too short. This looming societal anxiety only heightens our felt need to hurry, as though we must experience more since there's so little time. So many people look back on life in total shock and think, *Where did the time go?* This is ironic because hurrying through life is often the very thing that makes it feel as though life is going by faster.

If you want to feel as though life is going by slower and not faster, slow down your pace and experience new things. Your experience of time is completely relative. As we get older, time feels like it is going by faster and faster. This heightens our feelings of time-lack anxiety and causes us to hurry more. Most people don't know you can easily prevent the feeling of time going faster as you age.

New Experiences Keep You Young

Claudia Hammond wrote a wonderful book, *Time Warped*, about the psychology of time—that is, how we experience time faster or slower. The old view originally proposed ages ago by Pierre Janet was that it all had to do with ratio. The reasoning goes something like this: when I was five, a year was 20 percent of my life, but when I'm fifty, a year of my life is only 2 percent of my life. Ergo, the older I get, the less a year feels to me and is therefore experienced quicker because of relativity.

Hammond says that assertion has now been proven false. She says, in fact, studies show we all experience time the same in spite of our age—as it's happening. A bus ride feels just as long to a seventy-year-old as it does for a twenty-year-old. But our memories of life in general over long periods of time are experienced very differently. In other words, it's the weeks, months, and years that will feel vastly different as a memory depending on your age.[3]

There's a fix, though. If you want your overall meta experience of time to slow down, it's all about less stress and new experiences. Whether grand or simple, new experiences will seem to cause time to slow down. This is why a year goes by so slowly for a child. It's the first time they've seen that bird, the first time they've been to a library, the first time they've learned to read, and so on. This daily onslaught of simple yet new experiences causes the overall passage of time to go at a snail's pace. As we get older, and especially as we settle into our careers and habits, we tend to experience the same things over and over. If you go to the same places, doing the same thing over and over every day, life will fly by. But if you break those rote habits by doing something new, even if it's simple, you'll stretch out your perception of time. The weeks, months, and years will slow down. For example, on a road trip, usually the journey there will feel slower than the ride home. This is because on the ride home you've already seen everything.

Add stress to that rote everydayness, and time goes by at light speed. According to a study by psychologists Marc Wittmann and Sandra Lehnhoff, "The feeling that there is not enough time to get things done may be reinterpreted as the feeling that time is passing too quickly."[4]

Having new experiences to slow down your perception of time doesn't mean you have to go bungee jumping Saturday or partake of a litany of crazy events. Again, look at children. If you want time to slow down, you yourself need to slow down. Seeing something as simple as a new tree or taking a different route to work or meeting someone new in a different department at the office will cause time to slow in the same way seeing the Eiffel Tower would. New is new. In truth, we don't actually see many of the new things in life because we're going too quickly or looking at our phones. Going through life unhurried will cause you to notice things you would've never noticed before and will make you feel way less stressed. This will make your experience of life longer and deeper.

Many of us are like the boy and the golden thread. In this French fairytale, a boy who is impatient with everything is given a ball with a golden thread. The old lady who gives it to him says, "If you want something you don't like to pass quickly, just give the thread a little pull. Minutes will pass in seconds. And if you really want, pull harder and days will pass in minutes, and even harder, years will pass as though they were days."

The boy pulls this string through all his suffering, and within what feels like weeks he is an old man. Sorry for what has happened and feeling as though he's missed out on his whole life, he wanders back into the woods to weep. There again he sees the old woman.

"Did you like the gift I gave you?" she asks.

He says, "I liked it at first, but I used it far too much, and now I've missed out on my whole life."

The old woman answers, "Very well, I will give you one more wish. What would you have?"

"I wish that I could go back and be present through my suffering," the boy said.

> If you want time to slow down, you yourself need to slow down.

In a way, we have been given this same magic ball, but unlike the boy we will not have a chance to go back. The magic ball we've been given is all the distracting things that we use to avoid our difficulty and suffering. We hurry through many of the challenges that face us, use substances like drugs and alcohol, and turn to TV when life gets hard. But it's in our adversity that we grow, and it's there most of all we should be patient and present. Hurrying through life, including its many trials, will make existence feel shorter and less satisfying.

If a hungry lion is chasing you, hurry. If you need to rescue a dog from a burning building, hurry. But don't use the adrenaline your body creates for those "fight or flight" moments in life to check your e-mail.

That is in fact what many people are doing. When we find ways to pump up our adrenaline in order to be more productive and sharp witted, it can cause harm to the brain over time.

Too Hurried to Be Happy

Dr. Archibald Hart wrote extensively about this in his work *Thrilled to Death*. He found that there is an alarming uptick in what used to be a rare medical condition called *anhedonia*. Anhedonia is the neurological inability to experience pleasure. It's not the same as depression, but is more like a numb feeling in life. Dr. Hart says anhedonia is at all-time highs because of the ways people are hitting their brains with adrenaline. Whether it's constantly staring at bright screens that trigger this part of our brain or the constant stress and pressure we feel from work or school, millions of people in America have messed up the chemical makeup of their brain. The result is that the simple things that used to give them great pleasure, like a walk through the park or a conversation with a friend, fall flat and feel boring. This state is called anhedonia.

If this is you, don't fret. Dr. Hart says the cure is easy. Spend less time looking at vivid screens like your laptop, cellphone, or TV, and start forcing yourself to stop and smell the roses. Force yourself to enjoy simple pleasures. Do simple things like a bike ride or a hike, and be careful not to constantly hurry. You'll soon feel more energy and more pleasure in life.[5]

Hurry Hurts

Malcolm Gladwell wrote about a study done at Princeton Seminary that showed how hurrying could cause good people with the best intentions to do the wrong thing.[6] In this study there were two large groups of students. Each student was asked to put together a sermon on the Good

Samaritan, the biblical story about religious leaders—presumably the model of goodness and morality—who neglectfully walked past a beaten and injured man in the road and about the lowly Samaritan, a religious outsider, who was a "good neighbor" and helped him. These students were then to give the sermon to a large group at a nearby lecture hall.

As they were waiting to make their presentation in a room across the street from the lecture hall, students in the first group were told, "Oh, you're late. They were expecting you a few minutes ago. You better get going." To those in the second group they said, "Oh you've got a few minutes to spare, but you might as well head over early." Then they put an actor, dressed as though he'd been beaten and bloodied, right next to the back entrance where the students would go to give the speech.

You might have already guessed the outcome.

Of the group that was in a hurry, only 10 percent of the students stopped to help the mugged man. Many of these students literally stepped over him to give a sermon on the Good Samaritan. Of those who were heading over early, 63 percent stopped and helped the man. Those in a hurry vastly underperformed those who were arriving early. You cannot be in a hurry and be a compassionate person.

First Corinthians 13 is one of the most memorized and read Bible passages, especially at weddings. In his definition of love, the first thing Paul put on his list was "Love is patient." Or you could say "Love is not hurried." There's self-importance in hurrying. When we hurry, how can we see the hurts of other people? When we are in a hurry, how can we pray with someone or say an encouraging word that really means anything? Being unhurried means you are walking through life with a listening posture, listening to others and to the Holy Spirit.

Ronald Boyd-MacMillan spent some time at the feet of the spiritual father and one of the leaders of the then-persecuted church in China, Wang Ming-Dao. The spiritual father said to the student, "Young man, how do you walk with God?" Boyd-MacMillan listed a number of things that came to mind, such as studying the Bible and praying. Wang

Ming-Dao quipped, "Wrong answer. To walk with God you must go at a walking pace."[7]

Today, go against the habit of your heart to hurry, to worry, and to manufacture or control the outcome. Watch how—as you walk at the pace of Christ in a slow, trusting, and wise way—much good comes to you. You will be more productive, not less. You will be kinder. And you will have clear eyes to see the bright future in store for you.

13

YOU CAN TRUST YOUR FRIEND JESUS

We don't have the capacity to
exaggerate God's goodness.
—Bill Johnson

It is said that Jesus Christ is perfect theology. Jesus shows us what God is like. At no point did Jesus go around making people sick to teach them a lesson, not even those pesky Pharisees. He never said to them, "You den of vipers. I'm going to give you herpes until you get your act together. Get right and then come back to me, and we'll see if I take it away." Everywhere he went, Jesus was the embodiment of good news. He went around healing people and meeting their deepest needs. He taught his disciples to pray, "on earth as it is in heaven" (Matt. 6:10). There is no AIDS, death, hunger, or poverty in heaven.

So much of his teaching was getting his followers to undo the bondage of religiosity in their lives, to connect them to the blessing of heaven now. In fact, it was the Pharisees who taught that God made people sick as a punishment. Many of Jesus' miracles were done just to show people that this is completely false. The healing of the blind man in John 9 is just one of many examples.

In Luke 13, Rabbi Jesus was teaching in the synagogue. In the middle of the sermon, a woman who had been crippled for years came up to him and asked for healing. Jesus of course healed her. She straightened up and began praising God, and everyone got excited. The leader of the synagogue, who did not like this display one bit, got up in front of Jesus, turned his back to him, and faced the crowd.

"Everyone, everyone, come on now, it's the Sabbath. There's six days a week you can get healed from Jesus, but today is special. Just come back to him tomorrow if you want healing, but not today."

Jesus was furious. This was the kind of thing that made people think God cared more about rules than he did about people. He said, "You hypocrites! You take animals to get water on the Sabbath, but you won't allow this daughter of Abraham to be set free?"

The Bible says this "humiliated" the leaders. Why?

The Old Testament had some wonderful laws protecting animals. Even though you weren't supposed to work on the Sabbath, it was okay to take your animals to pasture and water. This is because not allowing your animals to eat and drink is animal cruelty. So here, when Jesus called this woman "a daughter of Abraham," he really put the choke on. He was asking rhetorically if God's people, those whom the religious leaders were supposed to shepherd, had less value than barn animals.

It's clear to me that one of the core teachings of Jesus again and again is that, despite what pastors and religious leaders may have told you in the past, God is for you. He wants you to thrive, he wants you healthy, and he wants you to be in a close relationship with him. In short, he wants you to trust him.

But Why Do Bad Things Happen to Good People?

The short answer about why bad things happen is pretty simple. Bad things happen because our world is partially cut off from heaven because of sin. Imagine that heaven and earth were bound together as one but then were torn apart by evil. God and his people have been constantly at work to bring heaven and earth together again. And it is happening. Christ will come again soon to finish this work.

As we live in the hopeful in-between, it's hard to understand why sometimes we get a miracle and other times we don't. The temptation is to say, "God did this bad thing," but I find that answer too simplistic. I think sometimes we must be okay with not having a good answer and simply living in the tension of mystery while holding tightly to what we do know. We do know that God is good and wants us well. That's reflected in the teachings and actions of Jesus. We do know that because of heaven, nothing can ultimately destroy us or our loved ones who trust in him.

I believe it is important to continue to pray for healing, renewal, and breakthrough and to keep believing for your miracle. That's in fact how Jesus teaches us to pray in the parables of the wicked judge (Luke 18) and the persistent neighbor (Luke 11). The overall message of both of those parables almost sounds like, "I don't know why he takes so long to answer your prayer, but don't give up. He's going to come through for you." So whatever you're going through, keep hope alive and trust in God even if it doesn't always make sense.

Two Orthodox Jews Who Changed My Life

Ages ago, when I was studying the doctrines of Calvin, Augustine, and especially Greek philosophers like Plato, I was going down a weird rabbit hole of bizarre overanalysis. One day, Hannah and I were in the LAX terminal waiting to board a plane to Israel when we were visited by two orthodox rabbis who wanted to get to know us.

We had several interesting discussions, first about the current state of the nation of Israel and eventually about the relationship between Judaism and Christianity. At one point I asked, "What do Orthodox Jews believe about predestination?" They looked at me and said they had no idea what I meant by that word. I said, "You know, if God knows every-thing and is all powerful, is everything not a bit like a clock, just doing ultimately what he designed? Did God plan for you to sit where you're sit-ting and for me to sit where I'm sitting?" I picked up a pen and dropped it. "Did God plan for me to pick up that pen and drop it?"

After a long pause (and I mean super long, like I wondered if they had already checked out) they both looked at me like I might be crazy. The one on the right shrugged his shoulders and in a slightly annoyed voice said, "Who can know such a thing?"

Those words changed my life. I mean it. It helped me so much to realize I could know God deeply without knowing everything about him. It's like I had to come to terms with the idea that I'm not going to understand it all, but that I can know this: God is good. He's for you. He's on your side. He's going to get you through this. "Who can know such a thing" became the comforting words I needed to get me through my rigorous studies without losing my heart.

There will be a day when we get it, but for many of us, that day isn't today, and that's okay.

Trust

Faith simply means trusting God and trusting what he says. Trusting someone you can touch and talk to is a lot easier than trusting in a God whom you can't see. Even if you believe in God and believe he is on your side, faith can be difficult because God is invisible. The journey of walking by faith is one that is incredibly rich and rewarding, but it also requires patience. The Bible says, "Faith is the substance of things hoped for, the evidence of things not seen" (Heb. 11:1 KJV). In other words, faith is the belief that what you desire from God can happen out of nowhere and nothing. In theology we call it *ex nihilo*. God created the whole universe from nothing, and he can change what is seen from what is unseen.

The weirdest thing about walking by faith is you don't always know where you are going. You just know it's good because the One who is taking you there is good. It compares to a best friend blindfolding you on your birthday and taking you somewhere. You don't know where, but it's probably going to be great (that is unless you don't have faith in your friend). Walking by faith is like this. It is not comfortable being blindfolded, but at least you know something good is about to happen. The Bible, after all, says we "walk by faith, not by sight" (2 Cor. 5:7 KJV).

When the going gets tough, you might be tempted to ask for clarity, "Hey, God, I trust you and all, but things aren't looking good. Can you give me some clarity on this?" Brennan Manning told a story about John Kavanaugh asking for clarity from a living saint. Here are his words:

When John Kavanaugh, the noted and famous ethicist, went to Calcutta, he was seeking Mother Teresa . . . and more. He went for three months to work at "the house of the dying" to find out how best he could spend the rest of his life.

When he met Mother Teresa, he asked her to pray for him. "What do you want me to pray for?" she replied. He then uttered the request he had carried thousands of miles: "Clarity. Pray that I have clarity."

"No," Mother Teresa answered, "I will not do that." When he asked her why, she said, "Clarity is the last thing you are clinging to and must let go of." When Kavanaugh said that she always seemed to have clarity, the very kind of clarity he was looking for, Mother Teresa laughed and said: "I have never had clarity; what I have always had is trust. So I will pray that you trust God."[1]

Constant Surprises

Following God means trusting him, even if it's not clear where he's taking you. Following God means believing he always has a great surprise in store. No matter how bad things may seem now, you've done this long enough to know he is watching, he is involved, and he has something great in store.

> Following God means trusting him, even if it's not clear where he's taking you.

A life of following God is one filled with constant surprises. In fact, as you take godly risks and walk by faith, your mind changes from dwelling on the bad things that could happen to dreaming about the next great things that probably will happen. This is called *possibility thinking*. You fall in love with all the opportunities and possibilities that life has in store.

Being followers of Jesus, we don't make demands upon him, but rather we trust that he is going to pour out blessing on our life as he promised. We don't know what it is, but we know it's good.

When we think about possibility and opportunity, all of life changes. Anticipating good will nurture your faith and build in your heart and mind the character to do great things for God. Simply letting your mind run wild and dreaming about what is possible is probably one of the healthiest things you can do to have more energy and joy. The mental exercise of daydreaming is a good one. There's nothing like picturing something unbelievable and then saying to yourself, "It is possible."

Falling in love with possibility will make all the difference in your life. On the other hand, there's nothing that can sink a project quicker than believing it to be impossible from the beginning.

POUDRE RIVER PUBLIC LIBRARY DISTRICT

Phone: (970) 221-6740

www.poudrelibraries.org

Wednesday 01 December

Items checked out to

Stoil, Susan V

TITLE Peace after Combat : healing the spiritual &

BARCODE 314920318197929sgcl

DUE DATE 12-22-21

TITLE NlrV Adventure Bible for early readers / features

BARCODE 33052016394225

DUE DATE 12-22-21

TITLE You are beloved : living in the freedom of God's

BARCODE 330210319712429anyk

DUE DATE 12-22-21

Impossible?

World-class mathematician George Dantzig recounted a story of being in a graduate class in statistics at Berkley. One morning he walked in late for class and saw two problems on the chalkboard. He hadn't heard the lecture and assumed they were the homework assignment for the week. So after class he went home and for days labored on the questions. It took him what seemed like forever, but he finally solved them. After about a week he took the answers to his professor and apologized to him for turning them in so late. His professor, Jerzy Neyman, told him to just leave them on his desk. Dantzig recounted he was nervous to simply leave his work on the desk as it was covered with all manner of papers and books.

Six weeks went by, and then, early on a Sunday morning, Dantzig and his wife were awakened by a loud, frantic knocking at the door. It was Professor Neyman, who exclaimed he, Dantzig, had done it! He'd solved two "unsolvable" problems.

You see, the problems on the board were not a homework assignment; they were examples of two unsolvable statistical math problems. Since Dantzig had assumed they were just homework and therefore solvable, he went right to work and didn't quit until he was done. Dantzig and Neyman went on to publish their findings. It was the beginning of a great career for Dantzig.[2]

When people tell you your dream is impossible, they are not doing you any favors. If you listen to them you will be significantly decreasing your chances of success. Walking by faith and being a possibility thinker means you can shrug your shoulders in optimism and say, "I don't know how it will work out, but it will." Negative people may be right sometimes, but it's hopeful visionaries who change the world.

Trip to Russia

When I was finishing high school, I had a dream to go on a mission trip to Russia. I heard about a summer-long trip to Saint Petersburg where

Christian teens would be working at an orphanage. I was invited to go and instantly knew it was for me. I absolutely felt I had to do it. At the time I didn't know for sure if it was from God, but it sure seemed like it. I got it in my heart that it would be possible.

The only problem was the trip was leaving in five weeks and each missionary had to raise his or her own money. The cost of the trip: thirty-eight hundred dollars. My mom was broke, and I had a job at El Pueblo Viejo Mexican restaurant making six bucks an hour. Hearing "thirty-eight hundred dollars" sounded like "a bazillion million dollars." The number for me at the time was so big it sounded like a joke. But I just decided if God wanted me to go, he would make it possible.

I mentioned it to my grandpa, hoping he might help a little. He didn't. Instead he gave me some advice. He said, "In all my life I've realized that there's no bill that's bigger than God. If you have the vision, the money will follow." I took that to heart and started raising money.

I had setback after setback. I washed cars and worked at the church campground but got less than minimum wage. I sent out letters with almost no response and even did this horrible thing called *penny driving* where you basically abandon all dignity and go door-to-door pan handling for your mission-trip money. By the last week I had scraped together less than a thousand dollars. I thought all was lost.

Then came what Tolkien coined the *eucatastrophe.*

Eucatastrophe

Tolkien loved to use the literary device of eucatastrophe. It's an eleventh-hour happening when you think all is lost, everyone's about to die, and then some amazing breakthrough happens to save the day and give a happy ending. It's Frodo being rescued by the eagles on Mount Doom or the fellowship down to the last man at Helm's Deep only to be rescued by Gandalf and the Riders of Rohan at the very last minute. Being in ministry all these years I've actually seen this happen a lot. Some of the great breakthroughs I've seen in people's lives are so unbelievably awesome you couldn't get away with it in an airport paperback novel.

The last week before the money was due I was feeling hopeless. I'd given my all and wasn't even close—until it happened. Out of the blue, envelopes with my name on it filled with cash just started showing up at our house. They were not in response to my letters, because the checks were not made out to the mission organization I was going with. They were made out to "Bobby Schuller" with "Congratulations" in the memo. I was flabbergasted. None of them showed up with a note, and I couldn't figure out what was going on. Even weirder, most of them were coming from people I didn't even know. I didn't even recognize the names. Every day it was happening, though, and I could see my little pile of cash getting bigger and bigger . . . until I crossed the impossible thirty-eight-hundred-dollar mark.

I finally sorted it out when one of these checks came in a card from my aunt that said *Happy Graduation!* You see, I didn't know it, but my mom had sent out hundreds of graduation announcements with my senior picture on it. It went to all her friends, all her cousins and second cousins, and aunts and uncles. I didn't even know she was doing it. If she told me I'm sure I just brushed it off. Who had ever heard of a graduation announcement?

So raising the money had little to do with my efforts. It had everything to do with my belief. If I didn't believe Russia was possible, I would never have signed up. By the time the surprise graduation money came, it would've been too late.

That trip changed my life and prepared me for ministry in ways too vast to describe. Had I not gone, I would have probably used my money to buy a gigantic Gateway computer that would no doubt be in a landfill somewhere right now. Instead, my life was changed forever.

"You Can See . . . with Your Hands"

In her TED Talk "For the Love of Possibility," Liz Murray gave a touching account of the life of Ben Underwood. Ben Underwood was a phenomenon. He was a blind man who was able to see using sound. Using echolocation like a bat or dolphin, Ben would make a clicking sound with his mouth and could move around new spaces as though he could see. Many scientists flew in from around the world to see this amazing gift in action. Today there are lots of videos online of Ben using this trick to "see" with his ears.

Murray said Underwood was able to do this because his mother gave him the gift of believing it was possible. At three years old, Ben Underwood had cancer in both eyes and had to have them removed. When he woke, terrified, he told his mom, "I can't see!"

The mother's reaction was beautiful. She took his hands and placed them on her cheeks. "Ben, you can see with your hands." Then she gave him her arm to smell and said, "Ben, you can see with your nose." Then she whispered in his ear and said, "Ben, you can absolutely see. You can see with your ears."

Because of this refusal to label her son as blind, he got the idea that perhaps he could use his other senses to see in a way everyone thought was impossible. Murray said Ben's mother gave him the ability to think of the possibilities. "He began to ask not, 'Why can't I see?' but rather, 'In what ways can I see?'" This positive view of life in the midst of adversity is what gave Ben Underwood the ability to become the phenomenon he is.

Liz Murray related this story to her own life. Hers is equally impressive to that of Ben Underwood. Murray grew up in a home where both parents were addicted to drugs, and by the time she was fifteen she was homeless, living on the streets in New York City. Both of her parents contracted HIV and died when she was in her teens. She recalled that both her parents were "incredibly loving," but just couldn't shake their addiction. She remembered how she had dreams in her heart to do great things with her life—dreams that slowly died as she slept every night in subway stations and parks.

What If

She said it all changed when her mother died. It was that particular day because the tragedy got her thinking about how quickly life in general could change. She said that though it was hard to explain, she knew if her life could change for the worse so quickly, it could also change for the better. This is where she said she "fell in love with possibility." She got the "what-if voice."

She began to ask herself, "What if I went back to high school?" She started going around asking schools to take her despite her truancy record. She was rejected at one after another but was finally accepted.

Then she asked herself, "What if I got straight As?" She did.

Then she really went for it. "What if I applied to Harvard?" She got in.

How to pay for it? "What if I got a scholarship?" After telling her story to the *New York Times*, they paid her way through Harvard.

Now she goes by Dr. Murray. Her life was changed because she refused to allow others to define for her what was possible. She fell in love with possibility.[3]

God Loves Dreamers

Walking by faith doesn't mean it's always going to make sense. It means you have faith in the character of God. And the Bible continually says that faith pleases God. I think being a dreamer and a hopeful visionary is the natural response to knowing that God loves to do what people say is impossible. He loves to break all the rules to dote on his children.

Wake up every morning dreaming about what could be possible for you, and your faith will grow. This is because you will see miracle after miracle. You will begin to see a pattern of God's annoying eleventh-hour timing—the God of eucatastrophe. You'll begin to have the joy of being surprised by all the good life has to offer, and you'll become an even more insane dreamer. You will bother all those other impossibility

163

thinkers. As you walk by faith every day in the fog of uncertainty, you will be less afraid because of your many achievements. So keep dreaming and have an overactive imagination. Build your dream, and your dream will build you.

14

SHARE HIS LOVE WITH THE WORLD—JOY

Being happy is altruistic.
—Dennis Prager

God loves you and wants you to have a happy life. He's proud of you, and you're doing a lot better than you think.

The way people treat us has a lot to do with the way we view God and the way we view ourselves. It's easy to feel guilty about saying no or about wanting to succeed. Many of these ideas are not scriptural but inherited from religious people or society. It's clear to me that heaven is where everything God wants done is done. And yes, people in heaven are happy.

Joy is a scriptural mandate. Joy is proof that someone is in tune with Jesus and his grace. Joy is holy. It's the fruit of the spirit, listed only second to the ultimate virtue of love. A life that is rooted in knowing God, knowing that God loves us and that we don't have anything to prove, is a life full of joy.

Get out there and enjoy your life. Every moment is a gift from

God. Every breath is a privilege and should be enjoyed. Don't spend another minute people pleasing. Christians serve others and help others. Christians are altruistic, but Christians are not boundary-less doormats. You deserve dignity and happiness.

Perhaps, looking back through this book, you're thinking to yourself, *I've done many or most of these things and I'm still out of energy. I'm not overworked, I keep my boundaries, and I connect deeply with my friends and with God, yet I'm out of energy.* Many people do a great job of living the Scripture like Jesus but don't feel the happiness and joy that many other Christians do. When I run into this I suggest acting out in faith by *releasing your joy.*

Every disciple of Jesus is filled with the Spirit and therefore totally filled with joy. It's down there deep inside even if you can't feel it. You are like a deep and wide well full of water, but the water of life has remained untapped. Because you have joy within, all that is left is to believe and tap the joy deep in your heart as you would tap a well.

Christian joy is the unique gift that separates Christians from the rest of the world. There is a certain kind of happiness you can almost see in a person's eyes when they know Jesus. When I see it, I will sometimes blurt out, "You're a Christian!" They always are.

The world doesn't understand, but it hungers for it. That's why happy Christians are perhaps the greatest tool in the world for evangelism. People want to be alive and they need to see it from believers.

Enviable Green Fields

It reminds me of when the huge drought was happening here in Southern California about fifteen years ago. Everything was dead. There were massive fires, and the government was asking everyone to take five-minute showers every other day. People started getting neurotic and scared, some even calling the police if a neighbor's sprinkler broke or if someone was washing their car too long. People needed water and were getting worried it would be this way forever.

Around that time, at the property where my dad had a church, we had the greenest fields you could imagine. I worked there as a handyman and was responsible for fixing odds and ends. The place was a full-blown ranch given to my dad by the Crean family when he'd wanted to start his first church. It also functioned as a religious school and retreat center. In the southern part of the property we had beautiful orange groves. The property totaled well more than three hundred acres, and you could see it sprawling right from the 5 Freeway, the largest highway in California.

Every day we ran our sprinklers. We had soccer fields, large flowering fields, hills, and groves, and all of them were green as Ireland. People would write in angrily, cussing us out. We had people literally drive onto the property to give us a piece of their mind.

Your joy is not in short supply. It is coming from a deep well that will never run dry.

I totally understand why people would be upset, but it wasn't affecting the city's water supply in the slightest. If anything, it was helping by not drawing anything. What they didn't know was that we had a huge water well, a massive store of millions of gallons of potable water. We weren't pulling from California's water supply or the city pipes. Rather we were taking from a literal limitless underground lake that only we could access.

Joy in a Christian is a bit like this. The world may not understand why you are so joyful, but they are curious. Some people might be sarcastic or even cynical about your joy. They don't understand you are not getting your joy from the same place they are. Your joy is not in short supply. It is coming from a deep well that will never run dry.

Your joy is in your body. Release it. It's your strength. It gives your life flavor and draws others to you and to Christ. Dig deep as though you were digging into the earth, and tap into it.

Act As If

You're going to hate this next line: *if you don't feel it, fake it.*

I've received lots of criticism for my view on happiness, but I believe so much of happiness is choosing happiness even when we don't feel it. I believe it because it works for me and for so many others. The "Fake it till you make it" theory is not original to me. It's original to addiction groups and cognitive behavioral therapy.

Addicts are taught to act like a sober person until they become sober. This practice helps people get into new rhythms of sobriety and to be around people who are not addicted. Cognitive behavioral therapists do the same thing with those who are struggling with depression. During training, they ask the patient to do the things they would do if they were happy, and very often this is all the person needs to snap out of a fit of depression.

In order to master your emotions, you will sometimes need to do things that are contrary to how you feel. In this way you train your emotions to go more in the direction you want. This doesn't work in all cases, but it does most of the time.

In the analogy of the heart being a well full of joy, faking it till you make it is like tapping that well or priming the pump. Doing the things you would do if you were joyful can be the very thing that gets the rivers of life flowing. If you've ever lived on a farm or some other property with a well, you know the well sometimes needs priming. If you pump and pump and nothing comes out, it doesn't mean your well is dry. It usually means it just needs to be reset. To prime a pump, all you do is pour a bucket of water down the pump, and presto, the pump works again.

Assuming you don't have chronic depression or some other issues requiring medical attention, this little trick is something that works for most people. The problem is when we don't feel joyful, we don't want to act joyful. It somehow feels wrong. The idea itself makes us feel angry. As you think of joy as a virtue, something that's good for your life and others, it might be good to press through and break your streak of boredom and self-pity.

The next time you're full of energy, anticipate when you will be out of energy, bored, or a little depressed. Be prepared, and it will be so much easier to break the emotions of apathy.

Fishing When You Don't Feel Like It

I used to do this with my summer boredom. Summer in high school was such an amazing time. I didn't know how good I had it. For much of the season I would have very little responsibility and would find myself drifting into all the things I'd been dreaming of during finals week. I would sleep in until noon, eat cereal, and watch TV for most of the day. Though at first this lazy-dog approach to summer felt amazing, I realized even then this wasn't good for me.

I had a dear friend and neighbor who loved to go fishing. He wanted to go almost every day. I loved it, too, but would often forget that when I was lying there on the couch watching *The A-Team* at one o'clock in the afternoon. One day, though, as we were fishing, I realized how enjoyable being out of the house and doing something like this with my friend was. I understood, "I should never say no to this to just sit around and watch TV." I decided every time he invited me and I had nothing to do, I would just say yes.

Almost every time he came over, I didn't feel like going fishing. It was Oklahoma, and the summers were hot and muggy. I was in my air-conditioned house. I didn't want to get dressed, and when we did go, there was always a lot of work cleaning the fish and the tackle. These were the things that would come to mind. But even though I didn't feel like fishing, I knew it would be better to go. So, because I'd made the decision when I was feeling good, I chose every time to get up, get dressed, get out the door, and make the most of my summer. Every time I was glad I did.

Much of life is like this. We can't let how we feel in the moment rob us of a life of joy. Sometimes we need to just get up, get to work, and fake it till we make it. Sometimes we need to just press through and do the things we would do if we were happy. Very often, that's all we need to feel happy.

Happy Is Holy

If you're religious, you might be feeling uncomfortable with all the times I'm using the word *happy* with the word *joy*. I believe an erroneous teaching has worked its way into the church, and that is the idea that joy isn't happy. It's as if joy is some inner thing no one can see, as though even though a person is sullen and depressed they have some sort of unseen inner joy. This is totally false.

First of all, the word *happy* is all over the Bible. You may not notice it because translators like to render it as *blessed*. *Makarios* is the Greek and *esher* is the Hebrew; both mean "happy." I find the translation *blessed* to be egregious. Even though *blessed* is an accurate translation, many will read it as "holy" or something along those lines. Most people don't interpret *blessed* as "happy."

The point here is the Bible teaches a great deal about how to have a happy life or the "good life." God really wants you to be happy. I hope it goes without saying that he wants you to be happy by living his way. But still, the point remains. Joy and happiness are a part of living in the Father's world.

Joy is happiness, and it cannot be hidden. It smiles, laughs, eats, sings, and makes jokes. Joy is obvious. It's not some stoic inner strength. It's mirthful, and it's attractive. It is the most alluring characteristic of Christian discipline.

Also, joy is holy. Nehemiah gives a great example of holy joy. In this story the Jewish people were returning to Jerusalem after a long exile in Babylon. As a part of the renewal of Jerusalem, Nehemiah built his famous wall, a sign that the Jews were back for the long haul and they planned to stay. There was a dramatic moment when Ezra, the priest, brought out the Hebrew Bible and started reading it to the crowd and they began to weep. Ezra rebuked them for weeping and told them to celebrate. Here's the passage from Nehemiah 8:8–11:

> They read from the Book of the Law of God, making it clear and giving the meaning so that the people understood what was being read.
>
> Then Nehemiah the governor, Ezra the priest and teacher of the Law, and the Levites who were instructing the people said to them all, "This day is holy to the LORD your God. Do not mourn or weep." For all the people had been weeping as they listened to the words of the Law.
>
> Nehemiah said, "Go and enjoy choice food and sweet drinks, and send some to those who have nothing prepared. This day is holy to our Lord. Do not grieve, for the joy of the LORD is your strength."
>
> The Levites calmed all the people, saying, "Be still, for this is a holy day. Do not grieve."

The Gospel Creates Joy

The famous line that has been made into many songs and hymns—"the joy of the Lord is your strength"—was in direct response to people weeping to be pious. They were rebuked because they were supposed to have joy. Notice the joy here is reflected as celebration, including food and drink with friends.

Joy is not only your strength. It's the proper response to the gospel. It is good to respond to life with laughing, healthy fun with friends, and great meals. Believing we must always be serious in church or anywhere else to be holy is completely false.

Jesus modeled this joy in his own ministry. Rabbis were not even supposed to associate with sinners, let alone eat with them. Yet he did it all the time, and it seems like he was having fun doing it. Jesus' own account of himself in Matthew says: "The Son of Man came eating and drinking, and they say, 'Here is a glutton and a drunkard, a friend of tax collectors and sinners.' But wisdom is proved right by her deeds" (11:19).

Wait. They called him "a glutton and a drunkard"? In no way was Jesus either of these, but he ate and drank enough that his accusers had something to exaggerate. Jesus loved people, loved spending time with people, and although it's not written, I believe he was laughing and enjoying his time with them. Jesus is the most joyful person in the universe.

Prime the Pump

Just as a virtue like love or patience requires effort and training, so does joy. To be a joyful person, you must train yourself by priming the pump, by doing joyful things even if you're not feeling it.

Granted, there are times you should grieve. Hurrying the grieving process after something like the loss of a loved one will make the grief last longer. Trying to get someone to "snap out of it" is one of the worst things you can do to someone in grief. It's good to have a soul-friend who can walk with you in your pain. Perhaps you can find a friend who has gone through something similar.

However, most people, most of the time, don't have a real, concrete thing they're grieving over. Is that you? We often want to make boredom or nonhappiness our default until something makes us happy. Turn that around. Decide to make your default happiness. If you don't have a reason to be unhappy, do your best to do the things you would do if you were happy. Call a friend to see if they want to do something fun. Smile at people you meet. Pause and say thank you in your prayers. Get to work on a hobby or project that gives you meaning or joy. The truth is you have joy within you. You just aren't feeling it. Priming the pump in these ways will help you realize that you already have it within.

I know what you're thinking. *That's fake.* I'll grant that. It's totally fake, but that doesn't make it wrong. Taking a shower is fake. If you have a headache, taking an Advil is fake. I'm willing to bet if you're in a bad mood and your neighbor comes to the door, you're going to pretend to be in a fairly good mood (as you should). Isn't that fake?

Why wouldn't you extend that common courtesy to your spouse or kids? Nine times out of ten, acting happy will actually make you feel happy and train your mind to stay happy over the long run. In that sense it's not really fake. It's a life hack.

If you have no reason to be in a bad mood, it's unkind to act that way. This is because people are considered rude if they act happy around a sad person. Imagine a room with ten friends who are all happy. They're telling stories and enjoying the time together. You enter the room sad. They can tell something is wrong. Should you consider them rude if they keep acting happy? Sure, if you have something you're grieving about, you should enter the room and be vulnerable and receive empathy. But if you just had a stressful day, go in there and fake it till you make it. You'll feel a lot better and you won't bring everyone down.

I know what some of you are thinking. *Fine, I just won't be around people if I'm such a burden.* Again, you're not a burden. You are a treasure. The reason you can't withdraw is because people need your joy. People need you because life is hard. They need to know you're okay. They need your smile and your encouragement. They want to hear your stories and want to share in your gifts. You are an asset to your friends and family, and they don't want to do life without you. Your joy gives them strength to get through the many difficult challenges of life.

So set aside your pride and train your heart and mind into joy. When you think of happiness as a skill rather than a circumstance, you can change the whole outlook of your life, your marriage, your parenting, and your work.

The Science of Smiling

Did you know faking a smile with another person is almost impossible? Even if someone forces a fake smile, it becomes real because the person they smile at usually mirrors back a real smile. This creates a smile loop. Your fake smile becomes real because you see the other person smiling. It's like yawning. If you see someone yawn, there's a good chance you will yawn. There's a decent chance you are yawning right now just reading this. Smiling works the same way. When you see someone smile, it's nearly impossible to not smile back, unless you're angry and grieving. Smiles are contagious.

This is good news, because smiling is really good for your health, even if you fake it. In an article written by Leo Widrich, he pointed to a number of studies about the positive effects of smiling. He said, "When smile muscles contract there is a positive feedback loop that reinforces our feelings of joy."[1] Even if you fake a smile often, you tweak your brain chemistry in the direction of happiness. You're giving yourself a joy advantage.

Another study showed there were several nondrug-related ways you could hit the brain's reward mechanism. The number two thing on the list, not surprisingly, was eating chocolate. What was the only thing that beat out chocolate as a happy trigger? Smiling. Even faking a smile will trigger your brain's reward mechanism and release happy juice. Widrich says that, "smiling reinforces our brain's reward mechanism in a way even chocolate cannot match."[2]

In a recent study Matthew Hertenstein, a professor of psychology at DePauw University, researched old yearbook photos going back to the forties and fifties. He broke them into two groups: those who had big smiles versus those who smiled very little or not at all. You can likely guess where I'm going with this. Without a doubt, those who smiled in their photos lived happier lives, had happier and more successful marriages, and had fewer setbacks than those who didn't smile.[3]

This yearbook study was influenced by another famous work commonly referred to as the "baseball card study." In it, they studied 230 photos of baseball players published in the 1952 Baseball Register. They broke them into three groups: those with big smiles, those with a sort of grin, and those who didn't smile at all. The findings were startling.

Those with big smiles lived on average seven years longer than those who didn't smile.[4] Smiling is good for your health.

You know you used to smile more. The average adult smiles twenty times a day. The average child smiles four hundred times a day. What happened? Has life been so hard for us all that we can't smile as we did when we were children? Jesus said, "Unless you change and become like little children, you will never enter the kingdom of Heaven" (Matt. 18:3). Could it be that part of that change is reclaiming the joy and laughter of our childhood?

You are a joyful person. Believe it and release it. You are full of energy and life. Let it come out. Let go of your pride. Let go of proving yourself to others. God takes pleasure in you and wants you to take pleasure in the gift of life.

You are so loved. Everyone is looking for love, but when you make mistakes you may wonder:

- *Am I really worthy of love and belonging?*
- *Does God really love me?*
- *Do people really love me?*

Out of fear of being unwanted, rejected, or forgotten, it's easy to find yourself in the exhausting trap of proving your value. It gets worse when you are embarrassed by your mistakes and shortcomings. You wonder, *Will I ever be enough?*

You are not what you do, what you have, or what people say about you. You are the beloved. You always have been, and you always will be. Know that you are loved, and build your whole life as a response to that one truth.

God wants you to know there's always a home for you. You are his beloved child. He knows you by name and cherishes that name. There's no amount of messing up that can take that away. You can always come home, and he will be at the portals waiting with open arms to embrace you.

ACKNOWLEDGMENTS

Y*ou Are Beloved* has been the book on my heart for years, something residing within me that needed to be birthed. It's a message that has been on my heart for so long that when I finally wrote it, it was as if—in Dallas Willard's words—I was letting balloons go into the sky. I'm so thankful to the many people who put this book in my soul and those who helped me get it out.

First, I'm so grateful for the life and ministry of Henri Nouwen who taught us all that we are the beloved of God. I never met him, but read all of his books many times; they were a great comfort to me. To my friend, Dallas Willard, who taught me the value of abandoning outcomes to God. Also, great thanks to a pastor of pastors, Bill Gaultiere, who helped me stay mostly relaxed through this process.

I'm thankful for Ami McConnell who helped me understand the value of proclaiming the creed over people, rather than defending it. A special thanks to Matt Yates and his team for walking alongside me the whole time and believing this work could be something special. And I'm tremendously grateful to the whole team at Nelson Books who believed in the heart of this book and wanted to see it in print.

Of course, I love my church and ministry, my other family. I want to send a special thanks to my staff at Shepherd's Grove and *Hour of Power*. They did their best to work around my schedule to give me the time to

ACKNOWLEDGMENTS

write this book. I'm especially thankful for my friends and colleagues, Russ Jacobson, Chad Blake, Robert Laird, and the one who keeps my life in one piece, Bonnie Balloch.

Finally, I can't imagine having done this without my partner in life and ministry, Hannah. She held down the fort while I wrote away. She's always believed in me and I've always believed in her. To my mom, Linda, step-dad Ron, and sister, Brittany, for all the times you've watched our kids to help our ministry and writing work. We love you.

ABOUT THE AUTHOR

Bobby Schuller is the pastor of Shepherd's Grove Church in Orange County, California, and hosts the internationally broadcast television program the *Hour of Power*. He is the author of *Imagine Happiness* and *Happiness According to Jesus*. Bobby holds a master of divinity degree from Fuller Theological Seminary. He resides in Costa Mesa with his wife, Hannah, and their two children, Haven and Cohen.

NOTES

Chapter 1: The Creed of the Beloved

1. Name has been changed.
2. Brené C. Brown, *The Gifts of Imperfection: Let Go of Who You Think You're Supposed to Be and Embrace Who You Are* (Center City, MN: Hazelden, 2010), 30–36.

Chapter 2: You Matter to Others and They Matter to You

1. Maria Popova, "A Simple Exercise to Increase Well-Being and Lower Depression from Martin Seligman, Founding Father of Positive Psychology," *Brainpickings* (blog), February 18, 2014, https://www.brainpickings.org/2014/02/18/martin-seligman-gratitude-visit-three-blessings/.

Chapter 3: You're Not What You Do As a Vocation

1. Brown, *The Gifts of Imperfection*, 16.

Chapter 4: You're Not What You Do Morally

1. Brennan Manning, "Brennan Manning Live at Woodcrest," YouTube video, published by "toddsters5," May 30, 2007, 3:52, www.youtube.com/watch?v=pQi_IDV2bgM.
2. Brennan Manning, *The Ragamuffin Gospel* (Sisters, OR: Multnomah Books, 2015), 17–18.

Chapter 5: You're Not What You Do—But You'll Do Great Things

1. Finley Peter Dunne, *Observations by Mr. Dooley* (New York: R. H. Russell, 1902), 240.
2. Mother Teresa, "Whatsoever You Do . . . ," speech to the National Prayer Breakfast on February 3, 1994, Washington DC, audio recording and transcription, accessed January 23, 2018, http://www.priestsforlife.org/brochures/mtspeech.html.
3. Amy Morin, "The Secret of Becoming Mentally Strong," TEDx Talk, accessed October 23, 2017, https://www.youtube.com/watch?v=TFbv757kup4.

Chapter 7: You're Not What You Have—But Gratitude Will Give You More

1. Lynne Twist, *The Soul of Money: Transforming Your Relationship with Money and Life* (New York: W. W. Norton & Company, 2003), 17–18.
2. Shawn Achor, "The Happy Secret to Better Work," speech at TEDx Bloomington, YouTube video, published, by "TED," February 1, 2012, 12:20, https://www.youtube.com/watch?v=fLJsdqxnZb0&t=377s.
3. Robert A. Emmons, *The Little Book of Gratitude: Create a Life of Happiness and Wellbeing by Giving Thanks* (London: Gaia Books, 2016), 71.

Chapter 10: You Don't Have to Worry

1. Roy Baumeister and John Tierney, *Willpower: Rediscovering the Greatest Human Strength* (New York: Penguin, 2012), 35–36.
2. Henri J. M. Nouwen, *Our Greatest Gift: A Meditation on Dying and Caring* (New York: HarperCollins, 1994), 66–68.
3. Tony Robbins, "Master Meaning," Robbins Research International, accessed January 23, 2018, https://www.tonyrobbins.com/leadership-impact/master-meaning/.
4. Doug DiSiena, telephone interview with author.
5. J. R. R. Tolkien, *The Fellowship of the Ring* (Boston: Houghton Mifflin, 1954), 274.

Chapter 11: You Don't Have to Worry—How to View Stress

1. Abraham Twerski, "How Do Lobsters Grow?", YouTube video, published by "CreateYourFutureLife," April 7, 2016, 1:30, https://www.youtube.com/watch?v=dcUAIpZrwog.

Chapter 12: You Don't Have to Hurry

1. John Ortberg, "Ruthlessly Eliminate Hurry," *Christianity Today* (blog), July 2002, http://www.christianitytoday.com/pastors/2002/july-online-only/cln20704.html.
2. Neil Postman, *Amusing Ourselves to Death* (New York: Penguin, 1986), 11.
3. Claudia Hammond, *Time Warped: Unlocking the Mysteries of Time Perception* (London: Canongate, 2013).
4. Marc Wittmann and Sandra Lehnhoff, "Age Effects in Perception of Time," *Psychological Reports* 97 (2005): 921–935.
5. Archibald Hart, *Thrilled to Death: How the Endless Pursuit of Pleasure Is Making Us Numb* (Nashville: Thomas Nelson, 2007), 163.
6. Malcolm Gladwell, *Tipping Point* (New York: Little, Brown, 2014), 5.
7. Alan Fadling, *An Unhurried Life* (Downers Grove, IL: InterVarsity Press, 2014), 14.

Chapter 13: You Can Trust Your Friend Jesus

1. Brennan Manning, *Ruthless Trust: The Ragamuffin's Path to God* (New York: HarperOne, 2002), 5.
2. E. Bruce Brooks, "Tales of Statisticians: George B. Danzig," Mass., Amherst, February 1, 2006, www.umass.edu/wsp/resources/tales/dantzig.html.
3. Liz Murray, "For the Love of Possibility," speech at TEDx San Diego, YouTube video, published by "TEDxYouth," December 16, 2011, 12:25, https://www.youtube.com/watch?v=dbleDqLdhaE.

Chapter 14: Share His Love with the World—Joy

1. Leo Widrich, "The Science of Smiling: A Guide to the World's Most Powerful Gesture," Buffer Social (blog), updated April 1, 2016, https://blog.bufferapp.com/the-science-of-smiling-a-guide-to-humans-most-powerful-gesture.
2. Ibid.
3. Melanie Haiken, "Your Yearbook Photo: Can It Predict Happiness, Divorce, Even Death?" *Forbes*, April 7, 2014, https://www.forbes.com/sites/melaniehaiken/2014/04/07/can-your-yearbook-photo-predict-happiness-divorce-death/#5f84a40a56ea.
4. Ibid.

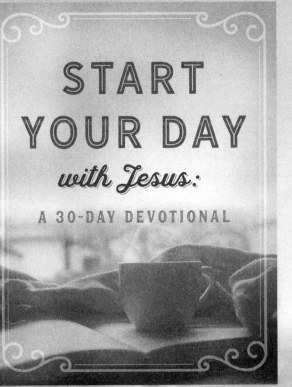